P9-AQI-192

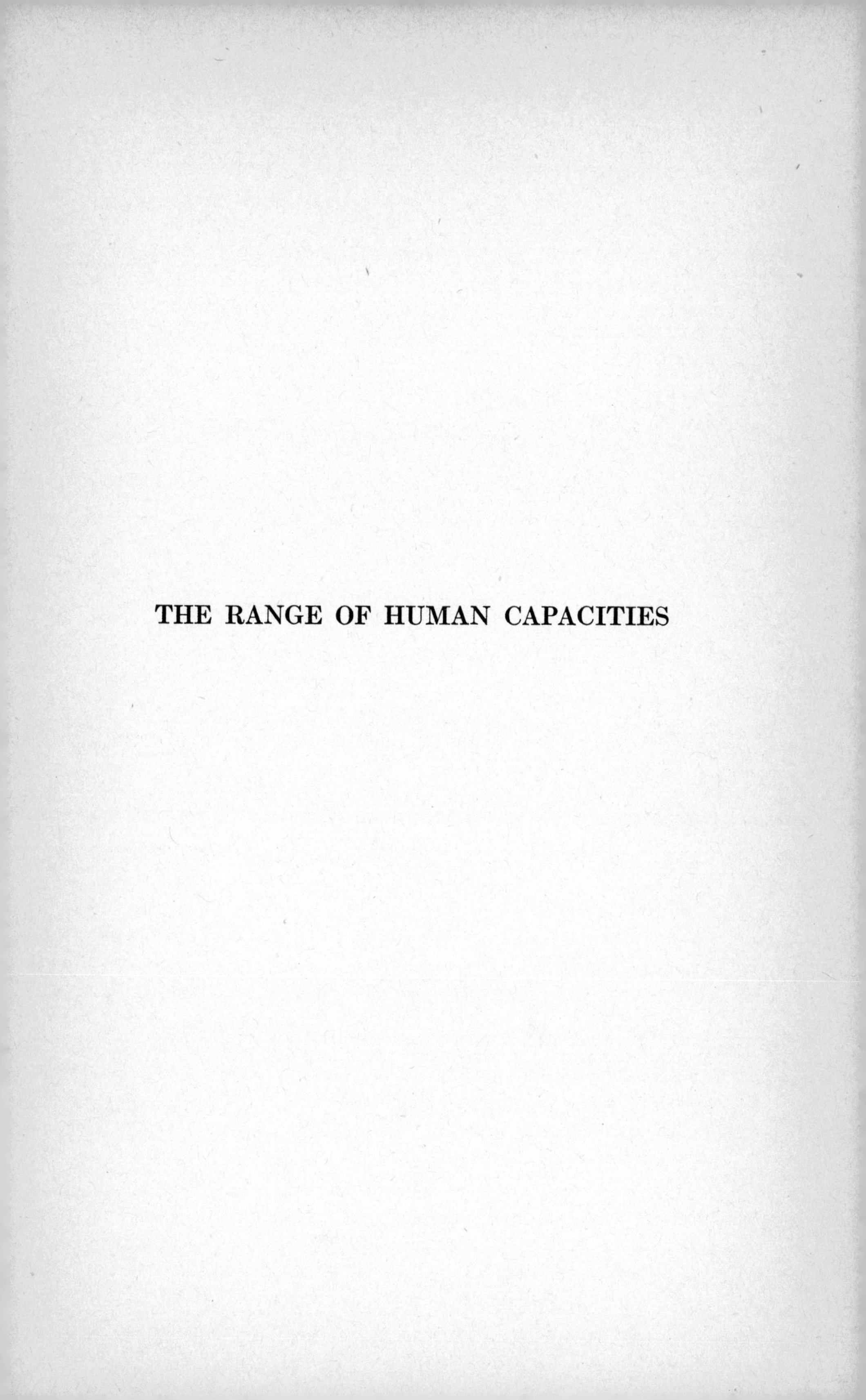

THE RANGE OF HUMAN CAPACITIES

THE RANGE *of* HUMAN CAPACITIES

By
DAVID WECHSLER, Ph.D.
Chief Psychologist, Psychiatric Division,
Bellevue Hospital, New York City

BALTIMORE
THE WILLIAMS & WILKINS COMPANY
1935

Made in the United States of America

Published September, 1935

Composed and Printed at the
WAVERLY PRESS, INC.
for
The Williams & Wilkins Company
Baltimore, U. S. A.

To

the undying memory of my wife, Florence Felske Wechsler, great artist and perfect woman, to whose love, genius, and inspiration, I owe the most joyous years and the most treasured possessions of my life.

CORRECTIONS

Page 41: Table 4, third column, second line of caption, change "between $M + \frac{\sigma}{\chi}$ to *between* $M + \frac{\chi}{\sigma}$."

Page 49: Table 5, *Stature*, sixth column (Extremes), change 152.6–164.9 to *194.9–152.6.*

Page 49: Table 5, *Sugar in blood*, sixth column (Extremes), change 116.0–182.0 to *116.0–82.0.*

Page 136: Line 10, change "Column 6," to "*Column 3.*"

Page 139: Table 9, *Stature*, sixth column (Extremes), change 152.6–164.9 to *194.9–152.6.*

Page 140: Table 10, *Sugar in blood*, sixth column (Extremes), change 116–182 to *116.0–82.0.*

Page 144: Table 13, *Weight of body at birth*, sixth column (Extremes), change 1,600–72.0 to *116.0–72.0.*

Page 145: Table 14, *Simple reaction time*, sixth column (Extremes), change 275.6–222.6 to *275.6–122.6.*

CONTENTS

PREFACE

In the following pages I have attempted to summarize our knowledge regarding individual differences, more specifically those aspects of it which bear on the limits and range of human capacities, and to draw such inferences from the data available as the facts seem to warrant.

Both the facts and the generalization may afford the reader some surprise, the former because many of the data collected will be treated in an unfamiliar way, the latter because the conclusions are for the most part at variance with current opinions on the subject. The reader will at all times be able to verify the facts by referring to the original sources from which they were taken. As regards the conclusions, the only suggestion I can make is that in evaluating them he lay aside, for the time being, any previous opinion he may have held, and seek to come to some conclusion himself in the light of the facts presented. I believe this effort will be amply repaid because the implications of some of the conclusions have, it seems to me, rather important bearings on a number of social questions with which thinkers all over the world are at present attempting to grapple. Outstanding among these, perhaps, are the status of democracy, the problem of technocracy in relation to human efficiency, and now, in a larger sense, the suggested attempts at social reorganization on the basis of abilities and needs as contrasted to geographical distributions and caste systems. I have not, myself, attempted to answer any of these questions, but I believe the material contained in this book should enable those who are concerned with them to approach the subject in a more scientific and, I might add, also in a more hopeful way.

D. W.

60 Gramercy Park,
New York, N. Y.

CHAPTER I

INTRODUCTION

When we compare the mathematical ability of an Einstein or the scientific intuition of a Pasteur or the poetic gifts of a Shakespeare with the correlative abilities of the average man, let alone those of a moron or idiot, the range of human abilities appears well nigh limitless. Are these seemingly large differences real or only apparent? Do men really differ so enormously from each other, or are these examples of genius merely isolated occurrences, flattering to be sure to the human species, but offering us but little information as regards the capacities of mankind as a whole? If the differences cited are so great as the extremes would seem to indicate, do they hold over the entire span of human capacities, or are they met with only in certain special capacities as, for example, that of mathematical or artistic ability? If they are not, by how much can, or more precisely, do, individuals differ from each other? How much faster is the fleetest runner from the slowest, how much more productive the most efficient than the least efficient individual in a given occupation? In short, is there a limit to human variability, and if there is, does the limit differ from one trait and ability to another, or is it equal in all directions?

This book is largely an attempt to answer the foregoing questions. The importance of the questions themselves, whether to the biologist in his study of heredity, to the psychologist in his investigation of individual differences or to the anthropologist in his evaluation of racial divergences, is perhaps too obvious to need special comment. But it may be well to point out, what may not be apparent at first approach, that the answers to them, far from being the concern of science alone, involve some of the most practical problems of human relationships,—of ethics, education, industry, and even politics. Thus, one of the main arguments of the eighteenth and nineteenth century philosophers for the establishment of democratic forms of government was based on the belief that all men were in fact, as Rousseau had proclaimed, created both free and equal, or, at least, with such insignificant differences of endowment as to warrant the universal franchise. This belief is at present very much in disrepute. Current social theory now favors government by experts, selected by an élite few; and this belief is seemingly based on the very opposite assumption that not only are all men not born equal, but on the contrary, with such varying degrees of endowment as to make the division of society into a ruling and a ruled class both natural and inevitable. Obviously, the answer as to which of these two views is correct can only be had from a knowledge of the actual differences in ability which separate the mass of mankind one from another, and not from any biased assumptions regarding them. The same holds for many other questions of social import, among them that of the uniform versus the sliding wage in industry; but before entering into any discussion of the practical implications of our subject, we must first consider its more general scientific aspects.

The main object of science is to discover the fundamental characteristics of natural phenomena and the invariable relationships which may obtain between them. One set of these relationships constitutes what are known as the natural constants. Examples of these from physics are the boiling point of water under standard pressure, the mechanical equivalent of heat, the value of "g" (the rate of acceleration of free falling bodies); in chemistry, there are the atomic weights and the special properties of the elements, their manner of combining, etc.; in astronomy, the mean distances of the earth from the sun and the other planets, their magnitudes and periods of axial rotation, and so on to many hundreds of constant numbers. Even more numerous than those in the physical sciences are those which occur in mathematics, of which, of course, the most familiar are the multiplication table and ratio of the circumference of a circle to its radius (π). But when we come to the biological sciences the number of natural constants actually calculated is relatively small, and that noted in psychology, smaller still; in the field of human capacities as such, their existence has hardly been considered. Investigators have been so intent upon showing how much people may differ from one another, that they have almost entirely neglected the problem of their likenesses. Nevertheless, there are definite limits to human variability, and these limits when properly determined reveal a constancy which, considering the data from which they are derived, is little less remarkable than that met with in the more exact sciences. The ratios between the extremes of ability have strikingly recurrent values which (when measured in a manner to be indicated later) fall roughly within the range 1.2:1 to 2.5:1, with a further probable maximum determined by the limit of organic rate of growth, namely the important mathematical constant, 2.712 . . . . . (e)

The whole problem of the range of human capacities necessarily hinges upon the definition of the word capacities and one's understanding of the term measurement. What constitutes a capacity, to what extent may such traits and abilities as body weight, strength of pull, arithmetical ability and general intelligence be compared, and in what sense, if any, may some or all be said to be measureable? These are not easy questions to answer, nor can universal agreement regarding them be expected. I believe, however, that they are not beyond solution, and these first chapters are accordingly devoted to a systematic analysis of the difficulties involved, and the various methods by which they might be circumvented. The solution offered is that human traits and abilities are measurable to the extent to which they may be expressed in terms or as functions of the basic units of physics or their derivatives, and comparable to the degree to which they lend themselves to such measurement. This is possible in the case of all physical traits, most physiologic and metabolic functions, and a small number of psychomotor, perceptual and simple intellectual traits and abilities. It does not yet obtain in the case of most abilities termed mental.

The cogency of any conclusion about the range of human capacities depends not only upon the validity of our concepts of measurement but also upon the reliability of the data to which they are applied. Our aim being to discover the distances which separate the least from the most able individuals in the general population, we must not only be in a position to measure the several capacities which we wish to compare, but be equally sure that the individuals measured will suffice to furnish us with the necessary data from which to obtain or calculate these distances. This means that certain statistical and logical criteria must be met, for example, that the group upon whom the measurements are made shall have consisted of a sufficiently large number of individuals, that they constitute a truly representative selection of the total population regarding whose limiting range one proposes to generalize, and so on. The application of these and other criteria of trustworthiness to the existing data on the measurement of human capacities greatly reduces the amount of material available for the purpose of our investigation. These data on the physical and mental measurements of men, all too sparse to begin with, except in the case of certain few anthropometric traits (like stature and body weight), dwindle down to a surprisingly small quantity when rigorously sifted. Some of the earlier published data are entirely unusable because their authors, even when making a sufficient number of observations, were generally content in expressing their results in terms of simple averages, rarely bothering to give any measures of dispersion, let alone the detailed distributions of their raw data which are necessary for the calculation of a reliable range measure. Again, as in the case of purely physiological and psychophysical measurements, the size of the groups studied have often been so small (under 20 individuals), that even where the full raw data were presented the inconsiderableness of the number of cases included makes calculation of any range measure of little statistical value. Finally, there is a large class of data which, though meeting the requirements both as to the fullness of presentation and sufficiency of number of cases (as well as other necessary criteria), nevertheless remain entirely useless for our purpose, because of the arbitrariness of the units in which the variables are usually measured. This is predominantly the situation in the case of educational and intellectual ability test results the original measures of which have seldom been made in terms of true units of amount.[1] Data from these fields will accordingly contribute but a relatively small part to our basic material.

While the paucity of reliable data and statistical inadequacies have greatly reduced the amount of material suitable for our investigations, enough remains to enable us to answer, at least in their broader aspects, the main questions which constitute our problem. To obtain this material has required considerable labor, not only because most of it had to be combed from what might be termed the farthest corners of periodic literature, but also because of the large amount of arithmetical work required to whip it into shape. In many instances it was necessary to derive the main constants from raw distribution tables, and in others to calculate them anew (as when the figures given were for non-homogeneous groups.) It is surprising how often even otherwise careful investigators will omit some essential statistical fact, and in the search for usable data, I had frequent occasion to wish that editors of scientific journals had made it a rule without exception to require authors of statistical studies to present their basic data in full.

[1] The problem of the measurement of mental capacities in terms of true units of amount is discussed in chapter II and the appendix.

The data from which the main conclusions are based are given in the tables to be found in chapters IV and V and in appendix B. The figures there given cover fairly exhaustively the principal available material published in the last thirty years, and I believe no important source has been omitted, although most of the figures have been derived from English publications. A certain amount of selection has been necessary. In general, where several sets of data for the same trait or ability were available, I have usually chosen for inclusion those based on the largest number of cases, without, however, neglecting such factors as the homogeneity of the group studied and the independence of the conditions under which the measurements were seemingly made. To avoid the frequently significant factor of age, the measurements included have been restricted to those of adults or definitely defined age groups; also, since comparable data for females are not always available, the measurements are mostly those of adult males. This in no way influences our final results, because while there is some slight difference of variability between the sexes, the difference between them as regards the total range ratios with which we are here concerned is practically negligible. The same is also true as regards the total range ratio difference between children and adults when the children's ages are kept constant. To show this a few sets of figures both for children and women have been included.

At the outset of these investigations, it was my intention not to use any statistics that were obtained from measurements of less than 500 individuals. It very soon appeared, however, that, if this criterion were closely adhered to, the investigation would have to limit itself almost exclusively to the study of simple anthropometric traits. It is regrettable but true that with the exception of such traits as height, weight, vital capacity and a few others, few of the capacities of man have been measured at all extensively. For example, while psychologists and physiologists have been measuring sensory thresholds for more than fifty years, there does not exist a single experiment in which as many as 100 individuals of any given age have been measured at any one given time; and the same may be said for most other basic psycho-physical and physiological capacities. The paucity of statistical data based on a large number of cases, however, proved to be less of a stumbling block than I feared it might be. A few trial calculations soon revealed the interesting fact that the total number of cases had far less influence on our range ratio than on the computed values of most other constants.[1] The total range ratio (of any given trait or ability) furthermore, showed itself to be relatively independent of such factors as age, sex and race when these were kept constant. For example, the total range ratio for stature of English female infants at birth differs very little from that of Egyptian male adults, ages 21–30. The only important source of error is lack of homogeneity, whether of the group measured or the conditions under which the measurements are made, and for this reason I have made this factor the main criterion for the inclusion or rejection of any given set of data. Nevertheless, with the exception of a few special instances, no data has been used in the tables unless based on the measurements of 100 cases.

The total range ratio which we shall use for the comparison of the variabilities of human capacities is the ratio between the highest and lowest, the least and most efficient individual of a measured population with respect to any measurable trait or ability, where the highest and the lowest are defined as the 2nd and the 999th individual in every thousand, respectively. The basis and validity of this measure of variability, as well as the method of its calculation, will be discussed in detail in chapters III and IV. Here, I can only state that it has been at once the inspiration and the basic concept of this investigation, and the one upon whose validity the cogency of much

[1] Providing, of course, the cases included a fair sample of the total population.

that follows will depend. By making it the measure of the range of human capacities, it will be possible, I believe, to show that human variability, when compared to that of other phenomena in nature is extremely limited, and that the differences which separate human beings from one another with respect to whatsoever trait or ability we may wish to compare them, are far smaller than is ordinarily supposed. The following pages are an attempt to justify this assertion.

CHAPTER II

THE MEASUREMENT OF HUMAN CAPACITIES

Much of what we shall have to say in this book will depend upon the validity of two assumptions: first, that the things we call human capacities may be treated as physical or psycho-physical quantities, and second, that these quantities are capable of measurement. It will therefore be useful to begin our inquiry with a definition of the word "capacities" and an analysis of the concept of measurement as it applies to them.

The general meaning of the word "capacity" is that of cubical contents, and in this sense is synonomous with "volume." This is its usual signification in physics. In anthropology and psychology it has acquired a number of altered and specialized connotations, although occasionally the original meaning of volume is retained. Thus, cranial capacity refers to the volume of that portion of the skull which contains the brain; vital capacity to the maximum volume of air which a person is able to take into his lungs; and similarly in a few other cases. But more often the original meaning of the term is only indirectly suggested. Thus, anthropologists may speak of body weight as a physical capacity. Since weight is measured in grams and not in liters, the term obviously derives its meaning from some implied analogy, the unexpressed relation seemingly being that the weight of the human body is to its cubical dimensions (that is, volume) as the weight of a vessel of water (or other standard substance) is to its volume. In other cases, the analogy is even less obvious, as when stature likewise is referred to as a physical capacity. In this instance, the use of the term may perhaps be explained on the basis of the fact that height often serves as an index of growth which in turn is classed as a capacity, but the original meaning of volume is no longer apparent. Such is generally the case when we come to the field of psychology. Here the term capacity has, to all practical purposes, become synonomous with the word ability. To the psychologist, reference to an individual's capacity implies the degree to which that person possesses a given trait or ability, that is, some quantitative or qualitative judgment as to the excellence of a function or performance. It is in this sense that memory, learning and reasoning are spoken of as intellectual capacities; speed of tapping as psychomotor, and courage, anger, etc., as affective capacities.

It is thus seen that the term capacity, as currently used, is applied to many types of facts or phenomena. If, in spite of their dissimilarities, these phenomena lend themselves to some common classification, they must of course contain a common denominator; in short, they must be alike in some way. There is in fact one way, and to my mind only one, in which body weight, speed of movement, memory, reasoning, ability to stand pain, etc., etc. are alike. They are all alike in so far as they are "measures of" certain qualities or quantities,—specifically, certain traits, functions and abilities in whose dimensions we are interested.

The object of this book will be to see how human capacities treated as "measures of" various traits and abilities compare with one another. This, of course, is not the only point of view from which they may be considered, and treating them as such, and only as such, will of necessity cause us to omit many facts of indubitable interest; but to my mind it is the only approach at present known by which the problem that confronts us can be scientifically envisaged. At any rate, it will be only to the extent human capacities can be treated as measurable quantities that we shall have anything to say about them. Such an approach, however, presupposes two conditions: first, that human traits and abilities are in fact measurable, and second, that the measures, in spite of the diverse methods by which they are obtained, permit valid comparison. Let us see to what extent these assumptions are warranted.

Our understanding of the problem will be facilitated by considering for a moment the nature and meaning of measurement in general. All measurements are primarily comparisons,—comparisons between the dimensions of a defined quantity taken as a standard and varying amounts of the same quantity whose relative dimensions we are seeking. The ratio between the two *is* the measurement. It states the number of times the standard or unit goes into the measured quantity. Thus, when we read that the Eiffel Tower is 300 meters high, the meaning is that if a length equal to that of a specially elected platinum bar, known as the standard meter, were laid off along its side, we should have to repeat the process three hundred times before reaching the top. Actually, of course, that is not the way we would go about measuring the Eiffel Tower, but that is the meaning our measurements would ultimately have to have, whatever the method employed. It is the same in the case of all other physical measurement. We choose a unit, assume that it remains unchanged throughout the process of measuring, and express the dimension obtained as so many multiples or fractions of the unit employed. Time is measured in terms of convenient multiples of the second, or the $\frac{1}{864000}$ part of the average duration between successive appearances of the sun on the meridian, known as the mean solar day; mass, by comparison with the gram, or one thousandth part of the standard kilogram which is the weight of a cubic deciliter of pure water at its greatest density; and so on of all other physical quantities.

Now, the selection of units and quantities in the manner indicated has two very important characteristics. In the first place, by definition, they are assumed to remain constant and equivalent throughout. The first and last inches of a mile are the same length, and the difference between 87 and 89 grams is equal to the difference between 518 and 520 grams. In using a rule you can begin at any point and always get the same result. The second important characteristic of the fundamental physical units is that they are generally, though not always, in substance or meaning, the same as the quantities they measure. A yard or a meter is really a piece of length. This is not true of all physical units. A degree of temperature as measured by the thermometer is not a bit of heat; it is a measure of what a certain quantity of heat will do to a substance, for instance a thin column of mercury; an ampere is not electricity, but the measure of the quantity of silver which an electric current will deposit in unit time. They are not disparate portions of a given quantity, but what in mathematics are known as functions, that is, measures of concomitant variation.

The derivation of units from functions instead of directly from the quantity itself at once introduces several difficulties. In the first place, it is necessary to know the mathematical expression of the function. You cannot select any single measure and then assume, as in the case of measures of length, that equal multiples of it will represent equal portions of the quantity, because the relation which exists between the quantity and its measure may be a very special one. The strength of an electric current, for instance, is measured by an instrument known as the galvanometer whose function is based upon the fact that when a current is passed through a wire, it induces about it a magnetic field. One of the simpler forms of this instrument consists of a circular coil of wire in the center of which is balanced a small magnetized needle which is caused to turn to one side or another whenever a current is sent through the coil. The degree of movement or deflections of the needle then become an index of the intensity of current passing through the coil. But it would not be possible to arbitrarily select a convenient deflection as a standard, and then assume that a deviation two times its size measured a current twice the strength, a deflection three times its size, three times as much, etc., because actually, the strength of the electric current passing through the galvanometer is not proportional to the linear magnitude of the needle's deflection, but to the tangent of its angle.

When units of measurement are derived from a function, it is necessary to know not only the exact expression of their function, but, if measurements of a wide range are to be made, to know it in its entirety, or at least to the limits within which comparisons will be made. For it is always possible for unlooked for changes to occur in any function at points not actually determined experimentally. This is well illustrated by the variations in Boyle's Law relating to the way in which the volume of a gas changes under different pressures. The general statement of the law is that for a given mass of gas, the temperature remaining constant, its volume will vary inversely as the pressure, or that the product (pv) of the pressure (p) by the volume (v) is a constant. This holds for small changes of pressure and under ordinary temperatures with sufficient approximation, so that on the ordinary house or mercury barometer, successive units of change are indicated by equal distances on the scale. But experimental studies on the compressibility of gases at different temperatures and over a wide range of pressures (as high as 3000 atmospheres) have shown that as the pressure is increased, the product (pv) slightly diminishes, and further, that when the pressure exceeds a certain amount (different for different gases) the product steadily increases, the higher the pressure employed. Here then a simple linear scale could no longer be used, because equal changes of volume no longer correspond to proportional alterations of pressure.

Now, the human capacities which we have set out to measure are in the main not simple quantities, but more or less complex functions. The numbers we obtain from our measurements are not ratios between parts or portions of the quantity we are really concerned with, but those of some other which is related to it in some special way. The quantity of material a person can recall or the number of digits he can repeat is not a particular amount of memory, but an amount of some arbitrarily selected quantity which is in some way related to, and hence assumed to be, a measure of it. This assumption is logically on a par with that which the physicist employs when he makes use of the magnetic effect of a current as a measure of electrical quantities, but differs in this important respect, that, whereas the physicist has already actually determined through experiment what the relations between the intensities and their magnetic influences are, the determinations still remain to be made in the case of most mental functions.

A detailed discussion of how psychologists have attempted to overcome the inherent difficulties of the problem of mental measurement would take us too far afield, and the interested reader must be referred to original sources.[1] We can only note here that while much has been done to clarify the problem, the fundamental questions involved have not as yet, in the opinion of the writer, received satisfactory answers.[2] These questions pertain both to the ultimate problem of psychophysical correlation and to the validity of the statistical methods by which attempts have been made to transmute what are known as scales of relative position into scales with equal units of amount. The latter question in particular has absorbed the attention of psychologists, and in recent years a number of methods have been suggested whereby such transformations might seemingly be realized. Expressed in non-technical language, these transformations consist essentially of statistical manipulations whereby the ability of an individual, instead of being expressed in terms of the original measures in

[1] See especially Boring (9a) and Thorndike (89, 90).

[2] The reasons for the writer's stand will be found in appendix A where the subject of the measurement of mental ability is discussed in greater detail.

which it was recorded, e.g., the number of items correctly answered on a given test, is given in terms of the degree of his deviation from the performance average of the group with which he is being compared, where the deviation itself is expressed as some fraction or multiple of some statistical measure of variability. The assumption behind this procedure is that equal multiples of variability may be taken as equal units of ability, an assumption to which, however, grave objections may be raised, and which, in the opinion of the writer, is ultimately untenable.

Summing up the work done on mental measurements, we must conclude that for most abilities we have as yet no adequate system of mensuration, and though the results of mental measurements may be frequently expressed by numbers, the quantities so expressed cannot be compared one with another in the same sense as physical quantities may be compared. We say only most, because there are a few simple mental abilities or rather types of performances which do lend themselves to such quantitative comparisons. These are the performances in which the evaluation of the difficulty of the task performed, or successive parts of it, does not enter into question. Such, for example, is the case when we measure a person's attention by asking him to cancel a single recurrent letter, for example the letter A, on a uniformly distributed page of mixed up print, and take as his score the number of letters checked in a given time; this condition is also approximately met in the measurement of simple reaction time, and, in general, in the measurement of all psychomotor functions where an identical or nearly identical task or element of a task is repeated, and either its duration or frequency of performance within a given time is the recorded fact. Certain aspects of memory[1] may also be measured in this way, but usually the

[1] Among these the writer would include memory span for digits. In this connection a distinction must be made between the intrinsic difficulty of successive elements of a task and the difficulty due to its spatial or temporal

more complex mental functions do not lend themselves to such treatment. For this reason and for others already stated we shall have to disregard the greater part of the data that has been published on mental abilities, even though many of them, to be sure, are given in terms of mental "measures."

In the case of physical capacities we shall have no such difficulties, because, for the most part, their dimensions are given to us in terms of the fundamental units of physics. Such at least is the case in the measurement of nearly all anthropological traits and of many physiological functions. In most instances we are concerned with lengths, or volumes, or weights, with an occasional measurement of force or velocity. We compare men as to height, length of their forearms, capacity of their skulls, body weight, strength of grip, rate of heart beat, etc. All these may be expressed directly in inches, pounds, or number per second. And we are accordingly permitted to make direct comparisons between our results, as in the case of ordinary physical measurements. The difference between 5 feet 4 inches and 5 feet 6 inches in man's height may be taken to be equal to the difference between 5 feet 8 inches and 5 feet 10 inches, as if they were successive distances on a metal rod; a pulse rate of 120 as being exactly equal to twice one of 60, because the thumps of the heart may be counted in the same way as the beats of a metronome, and so on. In brief, we may treat the successive units of our scale of measurement as quantitatively equivalent, and apply to them the fundamental processes of arithmetic.

---

sequence. For example, in the series 7–9–2–6–4–8, the number 2 is no more difficult to remember than the number 7 or 8, in the sense that a person with a memory span of six digits would not find it harder to recall the series if the numbers were reversed or placed in any other order. Psychologically, of course, the initial and last digits are "easier" in the sense that these numbers are more likely to be retained than those occupying a central position. But that has nothing to do with the problem of units of measurement, no more than the fact that the last yard of a race is the "hardest" for the runner alters in any way the fact that the first and last yard are of equal length. Psychologists have unnecessarily complicated their problem by failing to note this distinction.

To sum up, the problem of the measurement of human capacities imposes upon us several prerequisites. In the first place, it presupposes that the traits and abilities investigated lend themselves to quantitative evaluation. Second, not only must they be capable of quantitative evaluation but their dimensions must be such as may be expressed in terms of units which lend themselves to the ordinary processes of arithmetic. This means that the units of a measurement must be units of amount and not units of relative position or any other arbitrarily defined measures. But in addition to these purely arithmetical considerations there are other qualitative factors which must be taken into account. The most important of these are the conditions under which the measurements were made. For the purpose for which we shall have to use our data, the latter, though less concrete, are far from the least difficult elements to be evaluated, and accordingly, before we enter upon any comparison between the measures themselves, it is of some import to consider at length what the various factors are which determine their validity. The next chapter will, in part, be devoted to this task.

CHAPTER III

THE DISTRIBUTION OF TRAITS AND ABILITY

Human beings differ from each other not so much with respect to the kind of abilities and traits which they possess, as regards the degree to which they possess them. Indeed, if we omit such aptitudes as are clearly due to education and training, for example, a knowledge of Greek or the ability to drive an aeroplane, it may be safely asserted that there is no capacity which is not possessed by all in some degree, however small. On the other hand, even casual observation reveals that as we increase the difficulty of a task or extend the limits of a given trait the number of individuals who can perform the one or attain the other becomes fewer and fewer. The average healthy man under thirty can probably run 100 yards in 15 seconds, only the trained athlete can do it in less than 11, and the number who have ever done it in 9½ seconds may be counted on the fingers of one's hand. So also, we know that pygmies and giants are rare, and geniuses few and far between. But information of this sort is too gross to be of scientific value. It tells us but little of the actual range of human ability or its incidence at any given level. Here as elsewhere in science it is insufficient to speak of much and few and in-between. We need to know exactly how common the average man is, how rare the genius, how numerous the man who is neither one nor the other.

Our task then is to discover precisely how amount of ability is related to the frequency with which it is met. We start with the obvious observation that human beings will inevitably differ from each other by greater or lesser amounts, and propose to determine from an analysis of these differences the manner in which their capacities tend to distribute themselves.

This imposes two requirements. In the first place we must be in a position to measure with precision the trait or ability the characteristics of whose distribution we are seeking to ascertain, and secondly, the number of individuals so measured must be sufficiently large to permit adequate analysis of the data. Both of these conditions are unfortunately not always easy to fulfill.

The difficulties which the measurement of human capacities in general present we have already considered. It may be well, however, to add that our inability to obtain quantitative data is often due not so much to the lack of an adequate measuring rod as to the inadequacy of our knowledge of the thing we wish to measure itself. In many instances our knowledge of the trait or function with which we are concerned is as yet so vague that we are not in a position to measure it at all. Such, for instance, is the case of that part of an individual's make-up which we call his personality. So also, in the case of many traits to which we prefix the term "emotional." Nor does this limitation obtain, as is commonly supposed, only in the case of mental traits. The trait we call "susceptibility to disease" is a good example. We know something about the susceptibility of individuals with respect to certain specific diseases, but with regard to the tendency as a whole we are as yet in a fog. The chances are that we are here dealing not with a single capacity but with a very large number, many of them very complex ones, which might best be treated individually. Nevertheless, we are confronted with the fact that certain individuals are more prone to disease than others, and can indeed single them out, but are as yet too ignorant of the tendency as a whole to be able to measure it. In this our difficulty is no different from what we are confronted with in the case of personality. We can classify individuals as having attractive or repugnant or indifferent personalities, but what constitutes personality itself we are unable to state. Here again the probability, and indeed the evidence, is very strong that we are dealing not with a single, but with an interrelated series of traits; still, personality remains something which seems to characterize the individual as a whole rather than any particular aspect of him. Of such complex capacities, which we are admittedly in no position to measure, we shall have but little to say in the pages that are to follow. This may prove disappointing to many readers, because the capacities omitted from discussion are among those which are of greatest practical interest, but to have included them would have been mere pretense at knowledge where knowledge does not exist.

The second condition that must be satisfied before we can study the distribution of any ability is that there be a sufficiently large number of cases. The question of course is, how large. The general answer is, that that depends upon the character of the distribution itself and more especially, upon the number of factors that determine it. We should, for instance, require a considerably larger number of cases if we wished to determine variations in body weight among the general United States population, than if we restricted our inquiry to the weights of colored male infants immediately after birth.

The question as to what constitutes a sufficient number of cases has usually been considered a statistical problem, but while in its practical aspects it may be so, essentially it is a logical one. We make a series of observations and from the form of the data are required to state the probable law of their relationship, or what amounts to the same thing, of their distribution. Which is precisely what we do when we apply what is logically known as the inverse inductive method. Now, the number of cases which the inductive method requires for a valid inference is determined only by the number of terms, or as we might call them factors, which are combined in the proposition. Where only one related term, in our sense, one factor, is involved, three cases are logically sufficient; and indeed nearly all mathematical induction, where this is the case, is satisfied with four or five.

As an illustration, consider the simple geometric series, 1, $\frac{1}{2}$, $\frac{1}{4}$, $\frac{1}{8}$, $\frac{1}{16}$. . . . . What is the law which explains the order of the series? We know it at once by inspection, each succeeding term is multiplied by the same factor, $\frac{1}{2}$; but how does the mathematician arrive at, or as he prefers to say, prove it? The method is one of successive trials, or as Poincaré has so aptly named it, reasoning by repetition (raisonnement par récurrence). By actual multiplication, the mathematician finds it true in any one case, e.g., $\frac{1}{2} \times \frac{1}{2} = \frac{1}{4}$. If the factor is a correct one, then it ought to be true for any case; or, proceeding systematically and numbering each successive verification he would say: If true where $a = 1$, it ought to hold where $a = 2$. He tries it and finds that it does, and concludes that it is true for $a = 2$. If true for $a = 2$, it ought to hold where $a = 3$; actual multiplication shows that it does; hence it is true for $a = 3$; and so he might continue indefinitely. Actually, however, the mathematician does not do this. Instead, he proceeds forthwith to the "any-numbered" case, following the formula that if it is true for n–1, then it is also true for n.

The significant fact revealed by this illustration, is that the number of cases required to arrive at a generalization where only one variable is involved is very small. There is no advantage and it is not necessary to expand $(a + b)^n$ to 100 terms to prove the binomial theorem. But the situation is no longer so simple when we have more factors, or logically stated more terms to deal with. When we have two distinct terms their logical combinations allow four possible consistent relations;[1] with three distinct terms, the possible number is

[1] The number of possible logically consistent relations must, of course, not be confused with the number of possible arithmetical combinations. For fuller discussion of this subject the reader is referred to Jevons (42), chapter VII.

fifteen; with four terms no less than three hundred and ninety-eight. The number possible with five terms would be many times greater, and the task of ascertaining the exact number of logically consistent relations would be so laborious, that no one has actually performed it.

From what has just been said it probably will have already occurred even to the non-mathematical reader that the statistical description of an effect produced by any considerable number of causes (more than five), or to return to our immediate problem, the possibility of arriving at a distribution of a trait assumed to be the resultant of any but the smallest number of unknown factors, would not only presuppose the disposal of an almost limitless number of observations, but even assuming that we have them, presents a problem which hardly seems solvable. As a matter of fact neither the tools of logic nor mathematics, refined as they are, would enable us to solve the problem as stated. It is also a matter of fact, that practically we are able to determine frequency distributions of various sorts without actually having to make an infinite number of observations, and that mathematics does enable us to make these determinations as well as test their reliability. How this is possible, or the answer to this seeming contradiction, is to be found in the theory of probability.

The theory of probability, as Poincaré so beautifully pointed out, is one of the great paradoxes of our universe. It seemingly enables us to make valid statements about events in proportion to the degree of our ignorance of their complete causation. To illustrate: take the classical example of the distributions of errors (or deviations from the center) of shots directed against a target. If we assume that the deviations are due to the indefinitely large number of small but independent causes, the probable distribution of errors about the point aimed at may be readily calculated; if, on the other hand, we have in one way or another arrived at the information that the final dispersion is a resultant of five and only five definite causes mutually influencing each other[1] the problem becomes so complex that we are unable to determine the resultant distribution mathematically.[2] The reason for our predictive power in the first case is that we may look upon the final distribution as the mode in which a large number of successive events, each independent of each other may combine, and hence calculate from the laws of permutations and combinations the frequencies of the various events, and accordingly, by means of the infinitesimal calculus or the binomial theorem, the general form of their distribution. In the second case we have assumed five definite but undetermined conditions, and have set ourselves the task of discovering the resultant effect of their mutual interaction, a task which we have seen presents insuperable logical and mathematical difficulties.

It thus seems, to quote Jevons,[3] that "the theory (of probability) comes into play where ignorance begins." But the ignorance cannot be complete.[4] The theory further assumes, and this is its only inescapable assumption, that the causation of an effect, whatever its nature, be highly complex and, correlatively, that the differences that may arise from fluctuations in this causation be correspondingly small. This is a safe assumption for those variables with which we shall be concerned, namely human traits and abilities. There is little doubt that the things we call stature or body weight or intelligence are entities that have very complex causation, or to put it another way that they are produced by the combination

[1] And we have no way of "keeping them constant."

[2] For algebraically expressed, the problem involves the solution of an equation of the fifth degree. Mathematicians now generally accept the proof given by Abel, that solutions of equations above the fourth degree are impossible.

[3] Principles of Science, p. 200.

[4] In the absence of all knowledge, the probability of an event happening or failing is not $\frac{1}{2}$, as commonly asserted, but indeterminate. See on this point the lucid exposition of Prof. Cohen in his "Reason and Nature" (14), pp. 131–134.

of innumerable small causes.[1] So also are we justified in assuming that fluctuations in the causation of human traits will produce minute differences in effect, that is to say, that we may expect individuals to differ from each other continuously by imperceptibly small differences, for that, in fact, is what actual measurement shows to be the case.

But while on both theoretical and empirical grounds we are compelled to assume that the causation of what we call human traits is highly complex, the assumptions required by the theory of probability as applied to the calculation of frequency distributions, namely the independence of the individual factors and the absence of any inordinately preponderant ones, is not so sure. The difficulty which this uncertainty introduces is overcome in practice partly by the process of grouping, and partly by avoiding, either through choice of material or control of conditions, the factors brought to light by this grouping process. Thus, finding that stature is the result of two groups of facts which we term heredity and environment, we may eliminate the latter (at least in part) by including in our distribution only individuals of the same social and economic status. Or again, knowing that stature is a function of age, we can eliminate this factor by distributing the trait separately for each age. This is, of course, what the chemist or physicist does when he speaks of controlling the conditions of the experiment or keeping certain factors constant. Unfortunately "keeping conditions constant" in the measurement of human capacities is extremely difficult, among others, for the very important reason, that we are often completely ignorant of their existence. Nevertheless, there are a few which recur so constantly that they are worthy of special mention.

[1] Of course, causes are not simplified by the mere use of summary terms like heredity or environment. When we say that stature or intelligence is determined by heredity we do not hereby exchange a simple for a complex causation; what we call heredity is itself the result of a myriad determinants, and environment is but a summary way of saying "innumerable external factors."

The most obvious of these general factors which may influence the character of a distribution is that of age, and all but the most careless investigators have usually taken it into account. Nevertheless consideration of its influence has generally been limited to the studies of traits and abilities of childhood and youth, the most usual procedure being to consider all above 18 or 20 years as adults. Such gross demarcation may suffice in studies of certain static traits, as for instance, of the linear measurements of the body (stature, cephalic indices, etc.); in the case of most psychological abilities and physiological capacities, memory, general intelligence, visual acuity, vital capacity, blood pressure, to mention but a few, it would introduce serious sources of error. Indeed, as we shall show in a subsequent chapter, the abilities of old age, in many instances, correspond more to those of the preadolescent than to those of the average adult.

Two other influences which often affect distributions, particularly in the case of mental abilities, are education and practice (exercise). It would, for instance, be absurd to attempt to measure the intelligence of an illiterate community by means of the Binet tests, or for that matter any other test involving language. Indeed, we should have the same problem in a 100 per cent literate community, though to a lesser degree, because there is a strong positive correlation between amount of schooling and intellectual ability.[1] Similarly we could draw no legitimate conclusion regarding the distribution of vital capacity among the male population of the country as a whole, from the incidence, say, in its army (as has sometimes been done), for aside from the fact that soldiers are a physically selected group, their training as soldiers is such as to greatly increase the capacity, per se.

But by far the largest source of distortion is that produced by the fact that the individuals upon whose measurements our distributions have to be based, are inevitably a selected group.

[1] As measured by the usual types of tests employed.

In the case of human capacities we can never hope to measure but a very small portion of the total population regarding which we wish to generalize, and the problem is how to choose our cases that they may be truly representative. Statisticians are wont to offer rules and devices whereby the reliability of our sample may be tested, but useful as they are, not all the mathematics in the world can substitute for knowledge and native intelligence, and one might also add, intellectual honesty. Giving the standard deviation to three decimal places and showing that the difference in I.Q. between native Americans and that of immigrants of Italian extraction is more than four times its probable error, permits us no conclusion as regards the relative distribution of American and Italian intelligence, unless we know how representative of Italians in general are the immigrants of that nation, who have come to the United States. So also, a survey including every worker in a given industry (e.g. the steel industry) could still give a false conclusion as regards the earning capacity of individuals in that industry, if the survey happened to be restricted to an unusual period, for instance, the years 1917 and 1918, when wages were unusually high owing to the war.

Even the most unbiased sampling of a population is no absolute guarantee against the possibility of errors of selection, because all that can at any time be safely claimed for any method of approach is that no such sources of error were apparent so far as one was able to observe. This still leaves those influences of which we may not have been aware, and which later and more complete investigation may bring to light.[1] The number of ways in which time, space and circumstance may produce variations is almost limitless, and not only nature, but the processes of human institutions, social and economic are constantly resorting us. The sweat-shop no less than the equator is capable of altering the physical constitution of men, and it is well open to question whether re-

[1] A fact which the history of statistical investigation abundantly confirms.

ligion and caste have not done as much to stratify humanity as differences in native endowment.

The evaluation of the influence of selective factors on the distribution of human capacities is thus one of the most baffling as well as most vital of all questions which one has to face in dealing with the problem at hand. To explore it in any but its most general aspects, as we have done, would take us far afield. But, perhaps sufficient space has been devoted to it to show that in the choice of data upon which the conclusions of this book will be based, I have not been unmindful of the need of other criteria than those of mere numerical accuracy. Without further digression, therefore, I shall turn to the question which was to be our principal concern in this chapter, namely, as to how amount of ability is related to the frequency with which it occurs, and more especially, as to whether degrees of ability do, in fact distribute themselves in that symmetrical fashion which astronomers have found to characterize accidental errors of observation.

In discussing this topic, we shall find it useful to retrace the course which the statistician usually takes in arriving at the form of any distribution. His first step is the systematic arrangement of the measures made. The procedure consists of grouping the recorded measures into classes or class-intervals. For instance, if it be body weight that the statistician is studying, he will bring together into successive groupings individuals weighing between 80 and 85 pounds, 85 to 89 pounds, etc., although his original measurements may have been made to the nearest half pound. The size of the interval thus chosen is a matter of convenience; practically it will, in the main, be determined by the total distance between the extreme measures, and the number of observations available. Having decided upon his class intervals, the statistician next proceeds to tabulate and total the number of cases in each class interval, arranging these in some ascending or descending order. The orderly arrangement of data, in the manner just indicated forms what is known as a frequency table, and it is from such a table that the form of a distribution is determined. (See Table 1)

There are two ways in which the form of a distribution may now be described. The first and rough method is to transform the frequency table directly into a graph by laying off the numerical class intervals as successive linear units on an abscissa, the corresponding frequencies as proportioned heights or ordinates erected at the mid or terminal points of each

TABLE 1

Frequency distribution of lung capacity (white soldiers 66.5 to 67.5 inches in Height.)

Gould (31).

CUBIC INCHES	NUMBER OF MEN
Below 96	19
96–115	52
116–135	81
136–155	136
156–175	271
176–195	319
196–215	330
216–235	160
236–255	85
256–275	22
Above 275	16
N	1,491

class interval, and then joining the summits of the successive ordinates. Depending upon how the ordinate points or lines are joined, one obtains a "histogram" (fig. 1A) or "frequency polygon" (fig. 1B) or "smoothed curve" (fig. 1C), all of which, however, tell the same story, that is, give a rough graphic representation of the original numerical data. This simple method is the one generally used in everyday statistics, and considering the usual inaccurate character of such statistics, is perhaps sufficient for the purpose intended. But unfortunately, many who should know better go further than that, and assume that the form of the graph thus obtained gives an accurate representation of the relationship required, forgetting that one may with no greater surety draw conclusions regarding the true form of a distribution from such a representation than one can prove a proposition in geometry from the character of the accompanying diagram.

To ascertain the exact character of a distribution one must find the mathematical function which most accurately sums

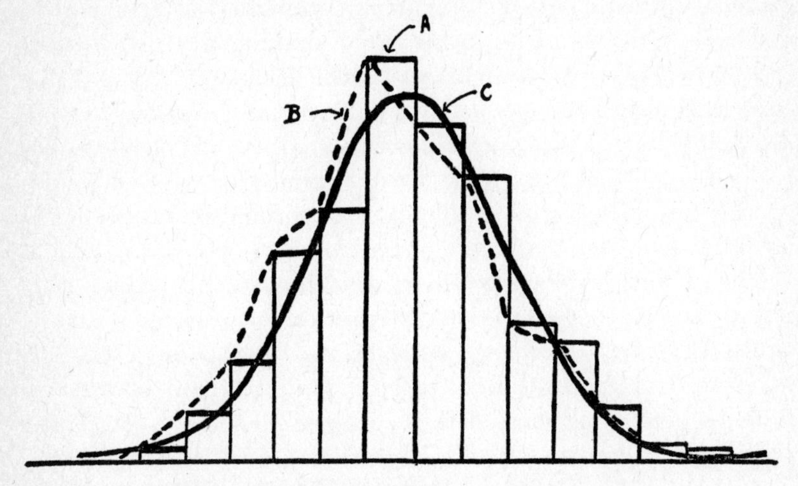

FIG. 1. (A) HISTOGRAM; (B) FREQUENCY POLYGON; (C) SMOOTH CURVE

up the relation between the two variables involved, namely, the exact manner in which the magnitude of a measure is related to the frequency with which it occurs. The technique involved in doing this is part of the branch of applied mathematics known as "curve fitting." With the arithmetical processes involved we need not here be concerned, except to mention for the benefit of those not acquainted with them, that the operation consists in finding the equation which will best sum up or fit the actual observations, or as the mathematician terms it, of finding "the best fitting curve" The process is somewhat laborious and presupposes a certain mathematical equipment, and for both reasons has generally been avoided by those engaged in practical statistics. Hence most of the conclusions met with regarding the distribution of traits and abilities must be regarded as sheer guesses, sometimes very good ones to be sure, but guesses nevertheless.

The first one who seems actually to have attempted a mathematical definition of the relation between the magnitude of human traits (measurements) and the frequency of their occurrence was the great Belgian anthropometrist and mathematician, Quetelet, who in his epoch-making work, L'Anthropomètrie (78), thus summed up this relationship: "The law of growth in man is expressed by the binomial which has become associated with the mathematical analysis of Newton and Pascal."[1] The expansion of this binomial gives what is known as the binomial form of the normal probability curve, the integral equation and more usual form of which we owe to Gauss. Quetelet was, however, the first to call attention to the similarity between the distribution of various measurements of man and those which Gauss and more especially La place had shown to hold true for random errors of observation. Quetelet illustrated this correspondence by comparing the actual heights of men with their theoretical frequencies, and after analyzing it, concludes: "The thing that especially merits our attention is that the distribution of human stature, much as it may appear to be a matter of accident, nevertheless obeys the most exact laws; and this characteristic holds not only for stature; it is observed not only in all measurements of weight, force and speed of man, but also in the sphere of his moral and mental qualities."[2] In this generalization,

[1] Loc. cit., p. 254. The original reads: "La loi de la croissance de l'homme est exprimée par la même binomiale que les travaux de Newton et Pascal avait deja attachees a l'analyse." The binomial referred to is the expansion of $(p + q)^n$ where p and q are the respective probabilities of an event happening and not happening, and more particularly, where p and q are equal to $\frac{1}{2}$.

[2] Loc. cit., p. 257. The original reads: "Ce qui mérite speciallment de

however, he was going beyond actual observations. In point of fact he had shown the generalization to hold only in the case of a few anthropological measurements. He did not at that time have the data required to test his hypothesis, nor indeed had he had them, would he have been in a position to do it rigorously, for want of the necessary mathematical tools. Here, as Professor Pearson remarks of him in another connection, Quetelet had "foreshadowed statistical advances without foreseeing the method by which they might be scientifically dealt with." The method was furnished by Professor Pearson himself.

There is no way of knowing in advance what the relation between the frequency and magnitude of physical and mental traits will be, and considering the infinity of mathematical equations which may, a priori, be applied to the same data, the reader can see for himself how important a task it was to devise a means whereby this relationship might be simply and accurately described. For the development of this method, we are, as already mentioned, largely indebted to the mathematical contributions of Prof. Pearson[1] who not only worked out the equations for most of the curves one is likely to meet with in practical statistics, but also furnished the researcher with a series of criteria which enables him to select from among the several equations the one that will most accurately sum up the data. These criteria form the basis of what we have above referred to as the scientific method of determining the form of a frequency distribution. They are certain quan-

---

fixer notre attention, c'est que les tailles humaines tant qu'elles apparaisent de la manière la plus accidentelle, sont soumises aux lois les plus exactes; et cette propriété n'est pas particulière à la taille: elle se remarque dans tous ce qui concerne les poids, la force, la vitesse de l'homme; mais encore a ses qualitiés intellectuelles et morales."

[1] These will be found scattered among the various volumes of the periodical Biometrika of which Prof. Pearson has been editor almost from its inception. Also the Proceedings of the Royal Society (see references). An early exposition of Pearson's Contributions in non-technical language will be found in his "Chances of Death and other Essays" (70).

tities derived from the ratios between various sums and products, known as the moments[1] of the distribution, the limiting values of which tell us which of the severally defined curves will best fit our data.

With these criteria available, the reader might well suppose that we ought now to be in a position to give a comprehensive answer to the question as to the actual distribution of human traits and abilities. Unfortunately this is not the case, the main reason being that, with the exception of the contributions emanating from Prof. Pearson's laboratory and the studies of some of his pupils, those who have been engaged in the task of gathering statistics in this field have devoted relatively little effort to the problem. Nevertheless, from the work that has been done the evidence is clear that, not only was Quetelet's generalization that the distribution of all or even most human traits conform to the normal law of error, premature, but incorrect.

Examination of actually fitted curves and frequency tables from which the general character of the distribution is definitely indicated shows that the distribution of human traits and abilities conform not to one but to several types of curves. The three principal types to which the vast majority conform are shown on page 33 (figs. 2A, 2C and 2D). Figure 2D is the familiar Gaussian or normal curve which Quetelet originally asserted, and which most text-books continue to cite as the universal form of distribution of human capacities. In point of fact, the only human distributions which are truly

[1] The moments of a distribution are the sums of the deviations of the individual measures from their mean (or other fixed point) divided by the total number. If "d" stands for deviation and "f" its frequency, the first four moments are given by the formulae:

$$M_1 = \frac{\Sigma fd}{N}; M_2 = \frac{\Sigma fd^2}{N}; M_3 = \frac{\Sigma fd^3}{N} \text{ and } M_4 = \frac{\Sigma fd^4}{N}$$

From these moments certain ratios known as β_1 and β_2 and K_1 and K_2 may be calculated, the values of which in turn serve as criteria for the determination of the best fitting curve.

Gaussian are those which pertain to the linear measurements of man, such as stature, lengths of extremities, the various diameters of the skull, and certain of their ratios like the cephalic index, etc. But even among these there is often a considerable deviation from true symmetry. In the case of most other physical and physiological functions, this deviation

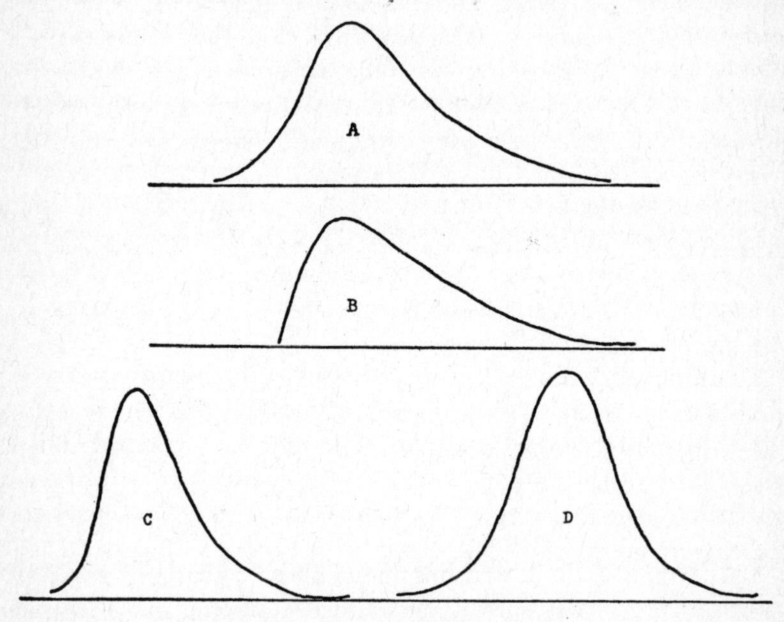

FIG. 2. FREQUENCY CURVES OF HUMAN TRAITS AND ABILITIES. (A) LIMITED RANGE IN BOTH DIRECTIONS (SKEW); (B–C) LIMITED RANGE IN ONE DIRECTION (SKEW); (D) UNLIMITED RANGE IN BOTH DIRECTIONS (SYMMETRICAL)

from the "normal" type, or skewness, is sufficiently great to call for another type of curve altogether. Body weights distribute themselves according to the curve shown in figure 2A, pulse rates in a type of curve shown in figure 2C, respiration in still another type, and so on. All that may be said is that occasionally one does come across a series of measurements of these functions which do roughly conform to or approximate a Gaussian distribution (e.g., Pearl's analyses of various brain weights). But one must hasten to add that such approximation is practically never met with in the case of the distribution of mental abilities.

The assertion that mental abilities do not distribute themselves according to the normal curve is contrary to the claim made for them in nearly all text-books of psychology where the question is discussed. Why the view that they do persists is one of those mysteries which only writers of text-books can explain. The fact remains that one finds precious few instances in the literature where frequency curves were actually

TABLE 2

SECONDS (t)	FREQUENCY
80	9
100	62
120	90
140	71
160	50
180	38
200	15
220	11

TABLE 3

RECIPROCALS ($1/t$)	FREQUENCY
125	9
100	62
84	90
72	71
63	50
56	38
50	15
45	11

fitted to mental data, and in none of these, so far as I was able to discover, was it shown that the best fitting curve was in fact the Gaussian type. In a number of instances the simple frequency polygons given, do seem to indicate that if a curve were fitted it would probably turn out to be Gaussian in form, but unfortunately these are precisely the cases where the method of measurement of the abilities involved is open to serious criticism. Such, for instance, is the case of many intelligence and educational "scales" where the practice has been to "weight" or re-evaluate the original test scores on the basis of their statistical frequencies. Naturally, in these instances, when the original test scores are redistributed they cannot but help give a form of distribution which the statistical artifacts employed, themselves served to produce. Accordingly the "evidence" from the field of mental and educational measurements must, for the most part, be carefully resifted.

In addition to the matter of statistical artifact, there are a number of other factors in the case of mental measurements, which may influence their form of distribution. One of these is the choice of unit employed. Thus, in measuring speed of perception, one finds that the distribution of scores is dif-

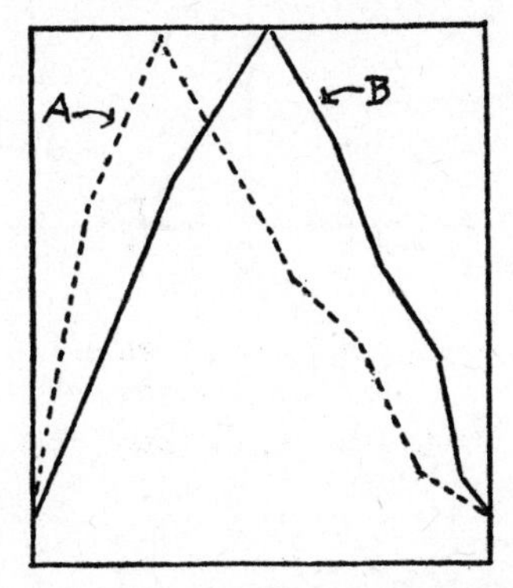

FIG. 3. FREQUENCY DISTRIBUTIONS ON CANCELLATION TEST WHEN (A) PERFORMANCE IS SCORED IN TERMS OF TIME REQUIRED TO COMPLETE TESTS AND (B) WHEN RECIPROCALS OF SAME ARE USED
(After Lazarsfeld)

ferent when the subjects' performance is measured in terms of total time required to complete a given task from what it is when its excellence is measured in terms of number of items perceived per unit time (see figs. 3A and 3B). Again the form of distribution obtained is dependent to a degree on the suitability of the material to the group tested with it (figs. 4A and 4B); also on the amount of practice which the individuals tested have had in doing the thing they are asked to do, and so on. A full analyses of these factors would take us too far afield; I mention them not with an intent at evaluation, but as a caution to the reader against uncritical acceptance of the frequently met with assertion that human capacities distrib-

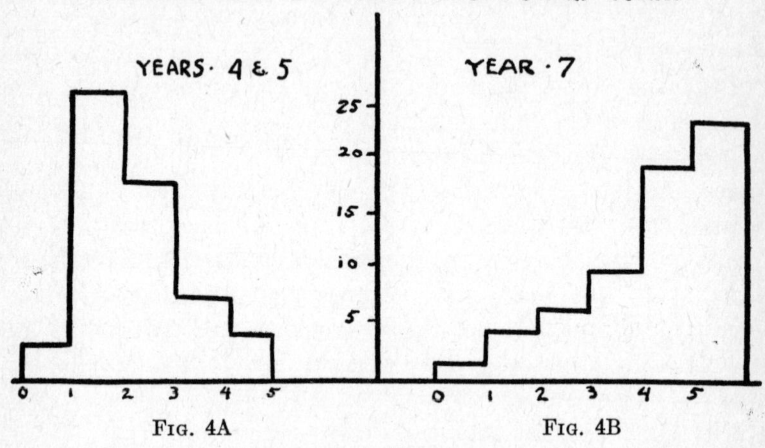

Fig. 4A

Fig. 4B

Figs. 4A and 4B. Influence of Difficulty of Task on Form of Dstribution

(Data from Pintner and Paterson)

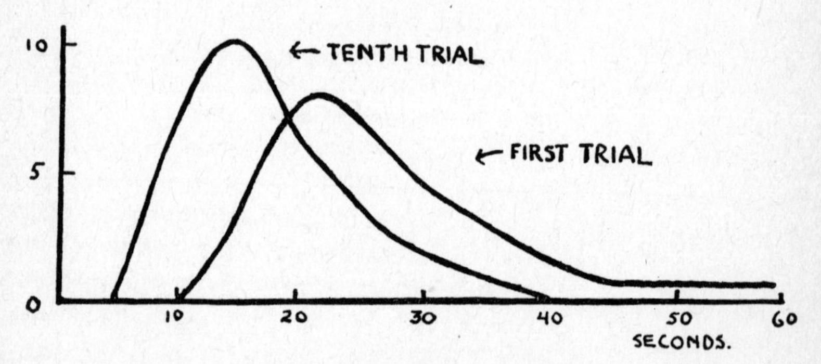

Fig. 5. Influence of Practice on Form of Distribution

(After Rupp)

ute themselves according to the normal curve. In point of fact the very contrary is more nearly true. Excepting the linear measurements, the distributions of most traits and abilities are definitely asymmetrical or non-Gaussian. This fact is important to us because it makes the task of estimating the limits of human capacities a much more difficult one than it would otherwise be. If we could assume that human capacities were always normally distributed, then, given a fair sample of measures, we should be able from our knowledge of the relationship of Gaussian constants to each other, to calculate the probable limiting measurements of the population as a whole. As it is, the ratios between the statistical constants obtained from distributions actually met with in practice often deviate so markedly from their theoretical (i.e., Gaussian) values as to lose both their validity and usefulness. Other measurements, particularly those of range and variability are needed. These will be discussed in the following chapter which is on the method of measuring the range of human capacities, and the first attack on our subject proper.

CHAPTER IV

THE RANGE OF HUMAN CAPACITIES

In our introduction we summarily defined the range of human capacities as that difference in ability or magnitude of trait, which separates the highest from the lowest, the least from the most efficient individual in a normal population. Concretely this means that if the measures of any trait or ability are arranged in an ordered series, the range is given by the numerical value of the interval or distance which separates the extreme or limiting cases. Thus, the (total) range of human stature would be the difference in height between the tallest and shortest individual recorded, expressed in inches or centimeters; of speed in running, as the difference in time required by the fastest and slowest individuals to cover a certain distance, expressed in seconds or minutes; of intelligence, as the difference between the highest and lowest test scores made on a particular examination, expressed in terms of the number of items passed, their mental age equivalents, etc.

This direct way of measuring range is open to several objections: There is first the obvious improbability that the least and greatest measures obtained in any given sample of population, however large, should in fact prove to be the true extremes of the population as a whole. If, for instance, in measuring heights of adult males, one finds in an even thoroughly representative group of ten thousand men, the extremes to be 4 feet 11 inches and 6 feet 6 inches respectively, the chances are very small that in another equally unbiased selection we would obtain the same figures. On the contrary, it is pretty certain that they would be different. They might, for example, be 5 feet and 6 feet 7 inches, and 4 feet 10 inches and 6 feet 3 inches, etc.; and while, by the theory of probability, we might calculate the amounts by which each could at most be in error, we could in no way be certain of what the actual limits were, until we had measured the entire population.

A second objection to the use of actually obtained extremes in the calculation of range is the greater individual unreliability of these measures due both to the fact that extremes more than any others are likely to represent errors of observation, and to the fact that they more likely represent instances which on the basis of general experience we have reason to reject as improbable. Thus, medical men usually reject the instances of extreme body temperatures which have from time to time been reported in the literature (e.g., of 112°F. and more); for, although such temperatures are not a priori impossible, they are so contrary to general experience and inconsistent with other physiological facts, that scientists are justified in assuming that these reported measures were biased by instrumental or other sources of error.[1]

Finally, measurement of range by the simple use of extremes is particularly subject to what may be termed the error of special factors. In the measurement of a group of individuals with respect to any given trait, the assumption not only is that all the individuals considered were subject to the factors which produced that trait, but abstracted from such others as may have affected only some and not all of the individuals measured. Thus, in measuring the amount of skin pigment in native white Americans we must be sure that the so called whites do not include superficially undistinguishable mulattoes; in measuring speed of running, of not including individuals with physical handicaps; in studying variations in "normal" temperatures, of seeing that our group does not include cases of "walking pneumonia," etc. Statistically this means that our group must be as far as possible homogeneous with respect to the particular trait which we may be measuring.

[1] In some instances they have in fact been shown to have been the result of tricks played by hysterical patients.

Such homogeneity is extremely hard to obtain in practice. We cannot, for example, be certain that our whites do not include very light mulattoes who have "passed," or that our runners did not include a case of incipient muscular atrophy or an individual who, during the course of the race, was seized with a cramp and said nothing about it, etc. All such cases may, by analogy to their designation in the field of medicine, be called pathological cases. The most serious limitation of calculating range by the simple method of extremes is that it makes no provision for the exclusion of these pathological cases, that is, instances which were clearly not intended to be included, and therefore ought be rejected.

For these and other reasons, anthropologists and psychologists have generally preferred to use other measures of range than that of the difference between extremes actually observed. A very common one employed is that of the interquartile-range, that is, the difference between the measures of the 25th and 75th percentile individual. This has the advantage of definitely avoiding the pathological individual, but the serious limitation of excluding 50 per cent of the entire population at the same time, a percentage far too great. This defect is in part avoided by extending the percentile limit in either direction, and some writers in indicating range have calculated it by using the difference between the 10th and 90th, or 5th and 95th percentile measures. But the more recent and more accepted practice has been to substitute defined multiples of statistical measures of variability, namely, the standard deviation, and more frequently, its derivative, the probable error.

The meaning of the standard deviation is dependent upon the type of distribution from which it is derived. As a general statistical measure it is defined as the mean square deviation, and is obtained by taking the square root of the sum of the squares of the deviations of each of the individual measures about their mean, divided by total number of measures. Its value as a measure of variability, however, is wholly contingent upon the form of distribution of the individual measures from which it was calculated. When their distribution is of a normal or Gaussian type, the standard deviation has certain special mathematical properties from which (the value of the S.D. and the mean being known) we are able to calculate within what limits certain measures will fall; and, conversely, given the limits (in terms of so and so many S.D.'s) what per cent of the total number of cases will be included between the

TABLE 4

$\frac{x}{\sigma}$	NUMBER IN 1000 INCLUDED BETWEEN MEAN (M) AND MULTIPLES OF S.D.	NUMBER IN 1000 INCLUDED BETWEEN $M + \frac{\sigma}{x}$ AND $M - \frac{x}{\sigma}$
1.0	341	682
1.5	433	866
2.0	477	954
2.5	493	986
3.0	498	997
3.5	499	999

Number of cases per thousand that can be expected to fall within certain limits of the average (mean) when the individual measures are assumed to be distributed according to the normal probability curve.

$\frac{x}{\sigma}$ represents fractional parts of the standard deviation when distances are measured in terms of it (S.D.).

defined limits. Thus, in a truly Gaussian distribution, a distance of 1 S.D., on either side of the mean, will include approximately 34 per cent of all the measures; 2 S.D., 48.5 per cent of the measures; 3 S.D., 49.85 per cent, and so on as shown in table 4. From which it can be seen that six times the standard deviation, taken symmetrically about the mean, that is, the distance comprised between plus and minus 3 S.D., will include almost all the cases, and could be very conveniently used as a measure of extreme variability.

The reader will now better understand why we devoted so

much space to the discussion of the form of distribution of human capacities, and in particular to the question as to whether or not their distributions conformed to the Gaussian parameter. If their distribution were truly normal, we should have in the S.D. a quickly obtainable and reliable method of calculating total range. This, however, is generally not the case. The distributions of undoctored measurements[1] of human abilities are predominantly skewed,[2] and often to such

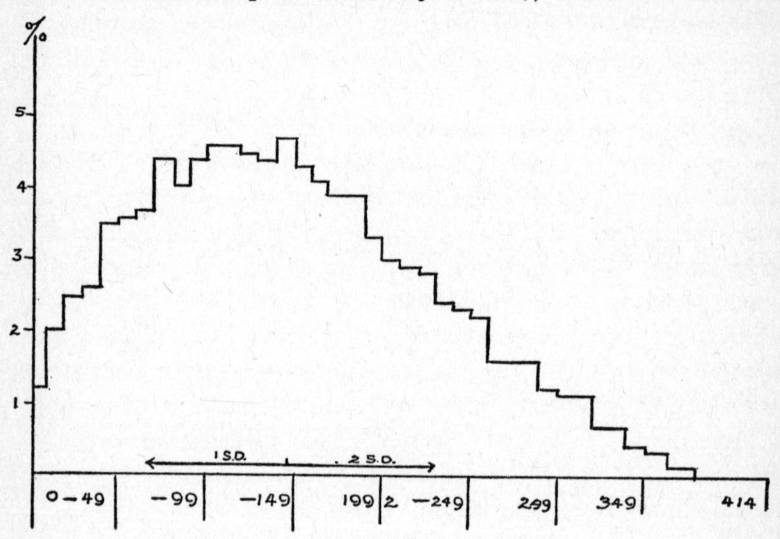

FIG. 6. DISTRIBUTION OF ARMY ALPHA SCORES (WHITE ENLISTED MEN)
(From Army Memoirs, p. 530)

a marked degree, that the use of multiples of the standard deviation as a measure of variability becomes both meaningless and erroneous. Thus, in the case of the Army Alpha Intelligence examination, the values −3 S.D. and −2 S.D. fall entirely outside of the distribution (fig. 6), and the measures M − 2 S.D. and M − 3 S.D. give the non-existent scores of

[1] By undoctored measurements, I mean such as have not been subjected to previous statistical transformations or arbitrary weightings.

[2] The exceptions have been noted in chapter VI.

−12 and −49.[1] Conversely, the calculated M + 2 S.D. and M + 3 S.D. scores fall short of their actual values. Thus, according to theory, the 84th percentile individual should have a score in the vicinity of 100, the 99th percentile of approximately 138; actually the obtained scores are more nearly 112 and 160, respectively. Clearly then, in the case of skewed distributions, and hence in the case of the distributions of most human traits and abilities, the use of standard deviation multiples based on the expectancies of the normal probability curve, will almost invariably give us incorrect delimitations of the true range or dispersion of the measures.

Our attack upon the measurement of range thus seems to have got us into a kind of dilemma: If we use actually obtained cases (i.e., the empirically observed extremes) to calculate the range of any given trait or ability, our results are likely to be vitiated by the inclusion of biased or unreliable measures; if, instead, we attempt to calculate their probable values from the theoretical expectancies of the normal frequency curve we run the risk of using unreal or non-existent figures. The dilemma however is more apparent than real; we have merely failed to consider all the alternatives. There is a way out: But before indicating the path, I wish to call attention to yet another problem with which the measurement of range question confronts us.

Let us first recall that what we wish to do is not merely to measure the absolute range of any given trait or ability, but to measure it in such a way as to be able to compare all with one another. The latter desideratum imposes the necessity of disposing of the particularity of the units in terms of which the compared traits and ability may happen to be measured. Concretely, we must find a way of comparing body weight, auditory acuity, intelligence level, etc., in spite of the fact that one is measured in pounds, the second in terms of vibra-

[1] The mean score of this distribution (white soldiers, native white draft) is 64.0; the standard deviation, 37.8.

tion frequencies, and the third in mental-age intervals. One way would be to reduce all the measurements to some common denominator, for example, to some basic energy unit. Unfortunately, this is not yet possible. The second way, and only other alternative, is to express our results as ratios instead of differences. For example, instead of saying that the range of body weight, however determined, was 160 pounds (the difference between the extremes 80 and 240), of auditory acuity as 2952 double vibrations (the difference between 5062 and 2110 d.v.), etc., one could express it as the ratio of the limits taken, that is, body weight as 3 to 1 (240/80), of auditory acuity as 2.4 to 1 (5062/2110), and similarly of any other trait or ability however measured. I suggest that the best way to express total range is by such a ratio, and propose that in the case of human capacities the limiting numbers used in the comparison be the measures of the 2nd and 999th individual in every thousand actually observed.

The ratio here proposed has hitherto not been used, and its introduction now requires perhaps some justification. The use of ratios as measures of variability however is not new, and a number of different ones have, from time to time, been employed. The most common and the one most in favor with statisticians is Professor Pearson's coefficient of variability. It is the ratio between the average and the mean square of the deviations of all the measures about it, that is, the mean divided into the standard deviation. The great merit of Pearson's coefficient of variation is that it gives weight to all measures, or what amounts to the same thing, that it is influenced by the idiosyncrasies of the distribution as a whole and not merely by the extreme ends of it. Where the question of the character or degree of variability of individuals about their average is the one which the investigator has in mind, this is probably the best measure available. But the question in which we are interested is not the degree of variability within a group but the extreme limits within which this variability takes place, namely, the thing we have called the total range. Now the total range of a distribution, as we have shown, can be approximated only indirectly from the variability of its individual measures, and then only if the distribution is of a Gaussian type; otherwise the figures so obtained will be both erroneous and misleading. Distributions having the same coefficient of variability may have very different limits, and conversely, distributions having identical total ranges may have very discrepant coefficients. It is thus clear that however useful the coefficient of variability may be for certain purposes, it cannot be used either as a substitute for or as an indirect measure of total range. There is, to be sure, a correlation between the total range and coefficient of variability ratio, and in a later paragraph I shall show how, in the case of traits and abilities whose distributions approximate the Gaussian curve, one may, by a simple formula, calculate the most probable total range of an ability from its observed coefficient of variability. But it is important to bear in mind that the two ratios measure two different and separate aspects of the variability problem.

With these considerations in mind, let us return to the definition of total range. Our original problem, we may recall, was to find a way to arrive at a measure of the limits of human variability by means of some measure which would at once comprehend the entire data upon which our calculations would be made, while yet avoiding the inclusion of biased and accidental measurements. This imposes upon us a further preliminary task of deciding when and with what degree of confidence one may reject actually recorded observations, a question which has engaged the attention of some of the world's greatest mathematicians (Legendre, et al.); and for which, it must be admitted, no universal solution seems possible. In specific cases common sense alone may be a sufficient guide. For example, in calculating the mean value of the velocity of light, astronomers now generally disregard the earlier observations made in this field, because these observations were made by instruments and methods whose accuracy in no way compares with those of recent date. But in the absence of specific knowledge we must rely on theoretical considerations, and it is here that the theory of probability again comes to our aid. The general rule which the theory offers us is to compare the probabilities of our entire data with and without the doubtful cases included and then reject or include these cases depending upon whether the validity of all is increased or decreased thereby.[1] Or, in the more precise terms of Pierce, from which the following is abstracted: "Observations should be rejected when the probability of a system of errors obtained by retaining them, is less than that of the system of errors obtained by their rejection multiplied by the probability of making so many and no more abnormal observations."[2] This rule, however, is not easily applied in the field of human measurements, and we must content ourselves for the most part with empirical approximations.

Starting with the premise, amply confirmed by experience, that biased and abnormal observations are more likely to occur at the extremes than in the middle or any other part of a series of measurements, one may reasonably conclude that the omission of the utmost extremes or at least a determined portion of them would in itself serve as means of ridding ourselves of the disturbing influence of the pathological case. There remains then only the calculation or determination of the actual per cent or portion of the extreme measures that may be dropped off without excluding instances which, (though deviating considerably from the central tendency of the series), ought nevertheless to be considered as normal variations. This is a matter of empirical determination. On the bases of my own observations I estimate that in the field of human measurements the portion of cases which may reasonably be

[1] For general discussion of this subject see Jevons (42), pp. 389–91.

[2] Jevons, loc. cit., p. 389.

dropped is not far from one to two tenths of one per cent of the total population, that is, approximately two in every thousand. If, then, we next agree to call abnormal all individuals who, with respect to any given trait or ability, fall within the lowest and highest tenths of one per cent of the population, the normal range of variability may be defined as the distance or interval of ability which separates the 2nd and 999th individual in every thousand measured.

I have chosen the interval 2nd to 999th individual per thousand as the measure of the limits of normal variability, and, consequently, their corresponding measures as the extreme values from which to calculate what we have defined as the total range ratio, for several reasons: In the first place, examination of empirical data shows that in many instances the per cent excluded by these limits corresponds roughly to the portion of population which, by criteria other than the measures themselves, constitute what may be termed the pathological or abnormal group. Thus, individuals who show blood pressures beyond the defined limits will almost invariably be found suffering from some pathological conditions such as lesions of the heart, hardening of the arteries, etc., that is, will be classifiable as abnormal by other criteria than actual measurement employed, although of course these may have served as clinical evidence. Similarly, individuals falling in the lowest tenth of one per cent of the population as regards intelligence may be shown to be mentally defective, that is, abnormal, by criteria other than by the statistical delimitations of intelligence based on intelligence quotients or tests passed, as for instance, by clinical or social standards, etc., etc.[1]

A second reason for the choice of the interval 2nd to 999th

[1] The converse of this is, of course, in no way implied. Individuals with "normal" blood pressures may yet have sick hearts, and persons falling, in our sense, within the "normal" range of intelligence may with good reason still be judged "defectives" on purely social or practical grounds.

individual per thousand as the limits of normal variability is that 99.8 per cent of the total population may for most purposes well be regarded what one might call the "mass of mankind," and it is the variability limits of the bulk of humanity which are the primary concern of this investigation. These limits are, of course, in a sense arbitrary, but no more arbitrary than any other limits that might be set. One may further concede that in some instances a percentage smaller (as seems likely, for example, in the case of body temperatures) or greater (as, for example, in the case of the incidence of mental deficiency) than the 0.2 chosen, more nearly represents the proportion of individuals or cases that must be regarded as pathological. But while it is not claimed that these limits are final or unalterable, one can assert on the basis of data on hand that they do not deviate to any considerable extent from those which more exact empirical data may be expected to establish. Finally, the definition of total range by the interval which includes all but the lowest and uppermost 0.1 per cent of the population has the advantage of corresponding to the generally accepted statistical measure of reliability, namely the quantity ± 3 S.D., which, as we have seen, is that distance which, laid off on either side of the mean of normal distribution, will include 99.7 per cent of all cases. In the case of distributions having a Gaussian or approximately Gaussian form, this correspondence makes it possible for us to calculate the total range of a given set of measures even when the number of cases available is considerably less than the desired thousand ordinarily required. The formula by which this can be done is given in appendix B.

I now come to what is the most important part of this book, namely, the actual data upon which all our conclusions on the range of human capacities must necessarily be based. These are given in detail in appendix B, tables 9 to 15. The data consist of an analytic summary of the means, standard deviations, extremes and total range ratios of 89 measured traits and abilities comprising the bulk of available data up to the year 1933. The data have been classified into six sub-groups, to wit,—measures of linear traits, measures of body circumferences, measures of metabolic rates, measures of physiologic functions, measures of motor functions, measures of the weight of the body and its divers organs, and finally, measures of

TABLE 5

Illustrative total range ratios of various human traits and abilities

TRAIT OR ABILITY	UNIT OF MEASUREMENT	NUMBER OF INDIVIDUALS AND DESCRIPTION OF GROUPS	MEAN	STANDARD DEVIATION	EXTREMES	RANGE RATIO
Stature	Cm.	96,239 white American soldiers	171.99	6.63	152.6–164.9	1.28:1
Sugar in blood	Mg. per 100 cc.	141 male adults	96.11	6.90	116.0–182.0	1.41:1
Duration of pregnancy	Days	245 German women	287.13	14.77	335–245	1.37:1
Chest circumference	Cm.	95,867 white American soldiers	88.99	5.18	108.9 –74.1	1.53:1
Blood pressure	Hg mm.	1,216 males, age 18 years	130.0	13.4	183.0 –87.5	2.09:1
Stringing discs	No. in 10 min.	200 boys, 14 to 15 years	41.9	6.2	55.0 –26.0	2.12:1
Weight of body at birth	Kg.	500 male infants	3.24	0.44	4.56– 1.92	2.38:1
Memory span for digits	No. correctly rep.	236 male adults	6.60	1.13	10.0 – 4.0	2.50:1

perceptual and intellectual abilities. Table 5 is composed of typical measures from each group to illustrate the method used in ordering the data and to indicate the central tendencies of the various traits and abilities as grouped. The figures which concern us in particular are those given in column 7, namely, the total range ratios, as above defined. Examination of these ratios very quickly reveals two outstanding facts, first, that the range of human capacities, when reduced to comparable ratios is always found to be a small number (by a small number I mean one that is less than five). Second, that a vast majority of the total range ratios (see tables 9 to 15) by which we agreed to define the range of human capacities fall within the limits of 1.3:1 and 2.5:1. In addition to these, they reveal still another important fact, one that is brought to light, however, only by a systematic classification of the traits and abilities into the various groups. This classification of the capacities (into linear traits, motor functions, intellectual abilities, etc.,) is to a certain degree arbitrary and not altogether exclusive, but, besides serving to bring together similarly measured types of traits and abilities, enables us to make the interesting discovery that the total range ratios of our various capacities (see tables 16 to 22) seemingly fall into natural groups or hierarchies. Thus the total range ratios of nearly all the linear traits fall between 1.22:1 and 1.40:1 (mean 1.30:1), those pertaining to motor functions from 1.65:1 to 2.50:1 (mean 2.33:1) those of perceptual and intellectual abilities from 2.30:1 to 2.85:1 (mean 2.58) etc. The mean and median values for all, together with their variabilities are shown in table 7 in the next chapter and in the tables of appendix C. To test the validity of the above results the reader will have to consult the tables given in appendix B, where the data furnished includes not only the source of the material but all such statistical information as make possible rechecking of the results obtained.

What is the significance of the findings to which we have just called attention? In the first place, there is an interest in them as a body of facts brought together now for the first time. Perhaps more important are the possible inferences which may be drawn from the data. The inferences which seem to me to be of particular moment are as follows: (1) The range of human capacities when calculated in true units of amount, is exceedingly small. (2) There are calculable limits to human variability which very probably are biologically determined. (3) These limits partake of the characteristics of natural constants. These three propositions are the main conclusions of the book; if correct, it is obvious that many of our current notions regarding the variability of human traits will have to be radically revised. It will, therefore, repay us to examine the inferences we have just made at greater length in order to determine whether they in fact merit the great significance which is here claimed for them. This will be done in chapters V and VI.

CHAPTER V

NATURAL CONSTANTS AND THE LIMITS OF HUMAN VARIABILITY (THE TWO TO ONE AND OTHER RATIOS)

If the reader has perused the tables in appendix B or even merely table 5 given in chapter IV, he cannot but have been impressed by several outstanding facts which the data there presented reveal. Some of them, like the smallness of the total range ratio numbers, their constancy about certain central values and hierarchial groupings have already been pointed out. I wish now to call attention to certain others, and to examine a number of inferences which our data, if valid, would seem to impose upon us. For this purpose I have remarshalled the original data, into a simplified and abridged form (table 6). The abridgment consists of omitting all but the essential facts necessary to our discussion and of combining certain entries in the original tables into single items, as, for example, using only one value[1] for the total range ratio for stature instead of three. This procedure is necessary in order to avoid giving greater weight to any particular capacity simply because several sets of data for it were available. Accordingly, every trait or ability for which we have measures, appears once and only once in the table irrespective of the number of times it is listed in the tables of the preceding chapter.

From an examination of table 6, the following facts are apparent:

Omitting the special case of body temperature and the two last items (Hard learning and Wt. of suprarenals), we find that the total range ratios of all the traits and abilities here collected fall within the limits of 1.16: and 2.93:1.

[1] The general method for combining data with regards to an individual capacity was to take the average, if only two sets of data were available, and the median, if three or more were available.

TABLE 6

Distribution of total range ratios

TRAIT OR ABILITY	RANGE RATIO	TRAIT OR ABILITY	RANGE RATIO
Body temperature	1.03:1	Respiratory rate	1.88:1
Calcium in spinal fluid	1.16:1	Platelets in blood	1.90:1
Urea in urine	1.21:1	Uric acid in blood	1.91:1
Length of head	1.22:1		
Breadth of head	1.23:1	High jump	2.01:1
Stature at birth	1.23:1	Rotation of eyeball	2.05:1
Haemoglobin in blood	1.25:1	Pulse rate (adult)	2.03:1
Calcium in blood	1.26:1	Blood pressure	2.03:1
Length of leg	1.26:1	Broad-jump	2.07:1
Adult stature	1.27:1	Speed of inserting bolts	2.09:1
Acidity of blood	1.29:1	Upper limit of audibility	2.09:1
Cephalic index	1.27:1		
		Stringing discs	2.12:1
Length of femur	1.31:1	Weight of healthy heart	2.14:1
Sitting height	1.31:1		
Height of sternal notch	1.31:1	Vital capacity (age and height constant.)	2.13:1
		Flexion of wrist	2.18:1
Heat of body (per surface area)	1.32:1		
Length of foot	1.32:1	Tapping	2.20:1
Span of arms	1.33:1	Simple reaction time	2.24:1
Duration of pregnancy	1.37:1		
Length of middle finger	1.39:1	General intelligence (Binet M.A.)	2.30:1
Interpupillary distance	1.40:1	Weight of body at birth	2.32:1
Sugar in blood	1.40:1	Weight of healthy kidney	2.37:1
Phosphorus acid in urine	1.40:1		
Circumference of calf	1.43:1	Weight of hair	2.40:1
Length of arms	1.44:1	Weight of body (adult)	2.44:1
		Simple learning	2.42:1
Heat of body (per kg. wt.)	1.50:1	Weight of placenta	2.48:1
Red corpuscles in blood	1.53:1		
Patellar circumference	1.51:1	Memory span	2.50:1
Chest circumference	1.53:1	Card sorting	2.50:1
O_2 consumption per minute	1.53:1	Latent reflex time	2.50:1
CO_2 consumption per minute	1.54:1		
Neck circumference	1.56:1	Weight of healthy liver	2.64:1
Thigh circumference	1.57:1		
		Vital capacity (only age constant)	2.75:1
Weight of brain	1.60:1	Intelligence quotients (Otis)	2.86:1
Cranial capacity	1.63:1	Swiftness of blow	2.93:1
Extension of wrist	1.65:1		
Running 60 meters	1.67:1	Hard learning	3.87:1
Pulse rate (at birth)	1.66:1	Weight of suprarenals	3.63:1
Weight of cerebrum	1.78:1		

If listed in order of magnitude (table 6), the total range ratios seem to be continuous, that is, show no wide gaps,—the largest difference between any two successive ratios (again omitting body temperature and Hard learning and Wt. of suprarenals) being only 0.11 points.

Nevertheless, more detailed analysis of the data shows that the total range ratios tend to group themselves around certain central tendencies. This is shown by the multimodal form of the histogram (fig. 7) which gives the distribution of the ratios. Part of the irregularity of the histogram is due to the fact that we have more of one type of measure (e.g., linear measures) than of the others (e.g., measures of perceptual and intellectual abilities) and part to the smallness of the total number of cases, but an examination of the listed traits and abilities definitely confirms this grouping tendency.

In order of magnitude, the mean total range ratios for the various groups of traits and abilities, are: Body temperature (in a class by itself) 1.03:1; linear measurements of body, 1.30:1; measures of metabolic rates 1.39:1; measures of body circumference 1.52:1; measures of physiologic function, 2.07:1; measures of motor coördination and speed of movement, 2.23:1; measures of body weight, 2.33:1; measures of perceptual and intellectual abilities, 2.58:1. The mean of these means is 1.92:1, and their median, 2.07:1. (See table 7; also tables 13 to 19.)

Observations such as the ones just noted led me, several years ago, to express the opinion that the range of human traits and abilities might be expressed by numbers which might be said to partake of the character of natural constants, and more particularly that these numbers or constants, when calculated in the manner indicated, tend to approach the ratio of 2:1. I now wish to discuss the extent to which the further investigations detailed in the preceding pages bear out these views. The two questions are not altogether unrelated; but for the sake of emphasis, I shall treat them separately.

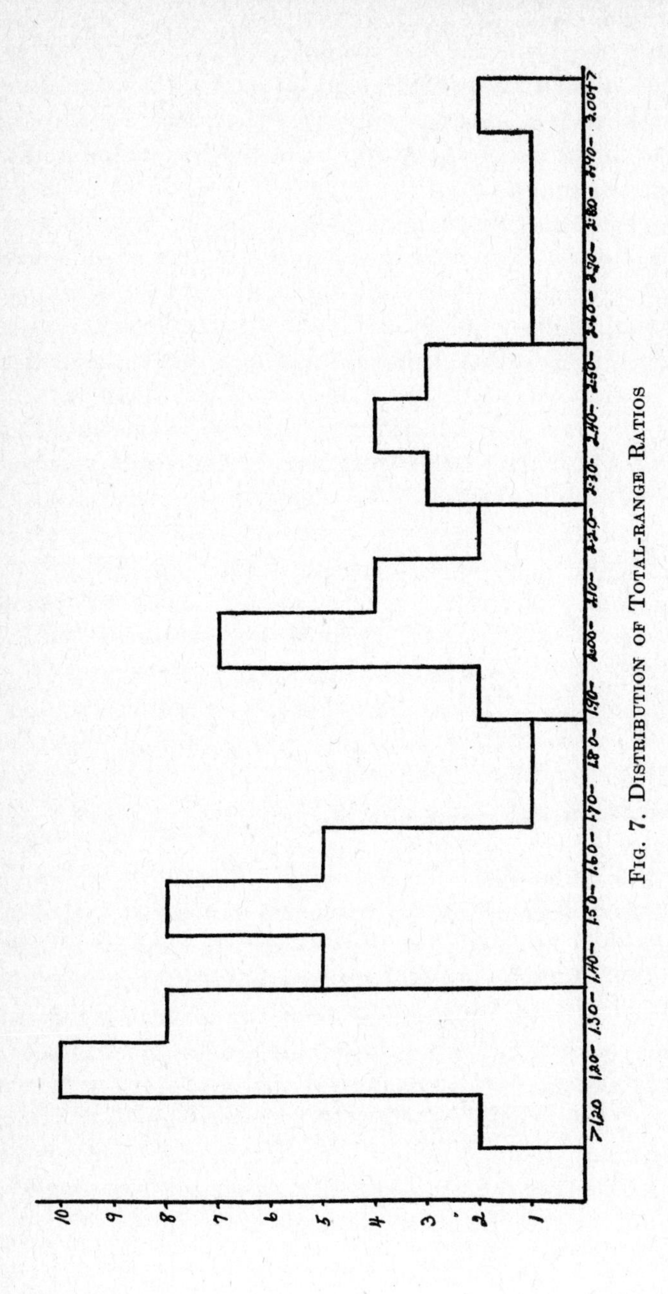

Fig. 7. Distribution of Total-range Ratios

Natural constants may be roughly divided into two classes: There are, first, those which are concerned with purely formal mathematical relationships. Such for example, are the trigonometric functions of angles, the ratio of the circumference of a circle to its diameter, etc., etc. These constants are characterized by the fact that they are unqualifiedly invariable and not verifiable by appeal to experiential evidence. In contrast to these, there are, second, the physical[1] constants, namely, those which purport to give the absolute or relative magnitudes of various natural phenomena or of the numerical re-

TABLE 7

Mean and median values of total range ratios for various groups of traits and abilities

GROUP	MEAN	MEDIAN	A.D.
Body temperature (N = 2)..........	1.03:1		
Linear traits (N = 13)...............	1.30:1	1.31:1	0.05
Metabolic rates (N = 18)............	1.39:1	1.41:1	0.16
Body circumferences (N = 5)........	1.52:1	1.53:1	0.04
Physiologic functions (N = 6).......	2.07:1	2.06:1	0.24
Motor capacities (N = 13)...........	2.23:1	2.17:1	0.22
Weight of body and organs (N = 10).	2.33:1	2.38:1	0.29
Perception and intellectual abilities (N = 7).........................	2.58:1	2.50:1	0.35

lations that may exist between them. Such for example, are the atomic weights of the elements, the value of the mechanical equivalent of heat and the measured velocity of light. These differ from the aforementioned mathematical constants both by the fact that they are generally[2] arrived at inductively

[1] In the wider etymological sense which embraces all natural phenomena, including the mental. The word "physical" literally means "pertaining to the (material?) universe and its phenomena," and is derived from the Greek "physis" = "nature" (from "phyo" = produce). Cf. Funk and Wagnall's Standard Dictionary.

[2] Though not always, e.g., Maxwell's determination of the velocity of light from his electrodynamics. A distinction must, of course, be made between a constant as a conceptual entity and a constant as an inductively determined fact, for example, between the atomic numbers as concepts and their values

from observed data, and what is even more important, by the fact that when so obtained are no longer invariable magnitudes but numbers which show a greater or lesser fluctuation about some mean value. Thus the value of G (the earth's gravitational constant) or even that of C (the velocity of light) unlike that of π, (the ratio of the circumference of a circle to its radius) is never given by a single number but a number with a plus and minus limiting value, its probable error. In the case of certain physical constants (e.g., that of C) the probable error is extremely small, in others (e.g., that of G) it is far from inconsequential,[1] but in any case the important point to remember is that as soon as we enter the realm of physical constants, we no longer deal with eternally invariable magnitudes, in the sense in which such are said to occur in mathematics.

It thus appears that when we speak of certain quantities in nature being constant, the constancy implied, however small their probable errors, is necessarily only a relative one. Actual measurements always reveal greater or lesser fluctuations about some central value, and the practical problem in each case is to decide how much of a fluctuation may be conceded and yet admit of the central value being classed as a constant. Different sciences, depending upon their exactness, have different criteria, but we must recall that even in so precise a science as physics, there is a marked difference in the order of variability (that is, relative probable errors) of its accepted "constants."[2] And these differences, it might be added parenthetically, would be even larger if physicists did not discard, justifiably to be sure, certain extreme values.

---

as experimentally determined. In the former case they are equivalent to mathematical definitions, and their exactness, like the units of measurement, once defined cannot be tested by experience.

[1] The respective values of these two constants as given by Birge (9), are: $C = 2.999796 \pm 0.00004 \times 10^{10}$ cm. sec., and $G = 6.64 \pm 0.01002 \times 10^{-8}$ dyne $cm.^2$ $g.^2$

[2] Compare for example the relative probable errors of C and G given in footnote 1. The latter has a relative probable error about 250 times as great.

The object of the foregoing remarks has been to recall the different meanings that may be attached to the term "constant," and to point out that in the case of natural phenomena, we must not expect invariable numbers of the kind posited in mathematics. When we speak of constants derived from actual observation, the meaning is always of a recurrent central (mean) value of limited variability. The total range ratios which we presented at the outset of this chapter seem classifiable as constants, in the sense that they partake of this essential characteristic. Furthermore, like all other natural constants, the limiting values of the measures are always of a restricted order of magnitude. Thus, while individuals may vary from, say, 4 to 7 feet in height, human stature is never such as to have to be measured at one time with a micrometer and at another with a surveyors tripod. It is always of the order of 10^2 cm. In brief, while we must freely concede that the total range ratios of human capacities are noticeably less fixed than most constants to be met with in physics, they can so frequently be expressed by central values of such limited range, as to merit inclusion among the relatively unvarying magnitudes of nature to which the term natural constants is so fruitfully applied.

Granting that the total range ratios which we give at the outset of this chapter partake of the characteristics of natural constants, there remains the problem of accounting both for the differences in degree of fixity of human as compared to purely physical constants, as well as for the differences in magnitude of the total range ratios themselves. As regards the smaller variability of the physical as compared to the human constants, part of the difference is obviously due to the greater precision with which the original measures necessary for the former may be made. But an even more important cause for this difference must be ascribed to the fact that the items which we sum up under the terms human capacities are much more complicated phenomena,—complicated in the sense that they are determined by many more factors. If this is true, then this fact alone would suffice to account for their comparatively greater variability, since the variability of any given phenomenon is necessarily the function of the product of the variabilities of the individual factors which determine[1] it.

The same sort of explanation which we may call the *multiple factor theory* will also account for the differences in degree of variability among the different human traits and abilities, themselves. Why, for instance, should the total range ratio for stature show a variability of less than one half that for body weight? Obviously, not because our measures of length are more precise or more accurate than those of weight, since in point of fact the balance is a much more accurate measuring instrument than a ruler. On the other hand, there are many influences which clearly influence the one and not the other. For example, adult weight is influenced by such things as food and water intake, both of which have no effect on stature whatsoever. If we look upon such influences as

[1] Many physicists might object to this conclusion on the ground that "physical constants are elementary and do not depend upon any factors." To which the reply is that, if it is objective data and not their assumption that is in question, the evidence is against them. This again brings up the question as to the meaning of measurement. Mr. A. W. Stern to whom I am indebted for this objection points out that apart from the natural limits to the accuracy of measurement (expressed) by the quantum uncertainty principle, physical constants themselves are independent of the inexactitudes of measurement, i.e., those due to experimental errors, etc., "because physical constants as such are as much a part of physical thought as are the physical concepts." All of which may be conceded, but again the answer is that there is a difference between the value of a constant as a concept and as a datum of measurement. So long as the physicist insists that his concepts are arrived at inductively he must be bound by objective facts. He may define a gram as an invariable quantity of definite amount but that does not mean that a gram of any specified portion of matter will always weigh the same. Certainly a gram of radium will not. To say that a gram of radium a thousand years hence will no longer be the same, is only begging the question. Nature is in a constant flux, and its elements are continuously acting upon each other. Part of the variability of measurement is due to the moment to moment alterations in all matter.

contributing factors, one may sum up the situation by stating that body weight is more variable than stature because it is a function of a greater number of factors. This point of view first suggested itself to me when my attention was called to the fact that the total range ratio for weight was approximately the cube of that of stature. This is clearly seen by comparing mean values for the total range ratios given for the two in table 6, which are respectively 1.27 and 2.44. If one considers the human body roughly as an elongated rectangular prism and allowance is made for the difference between the specific gravity of water and that of the body, its mass may be expressed as the cube of one of its linear dimensions. This suggests that, if it were possible to find certain other traits whose measurements were some dimensional power of another, one might further test the hypothesis by noting whether or not the total range ratios of the traits were to each other as their respective dimensions. Such an opportunity is afforded, in part, by comparing the variability of simple linear measurements of the body with those which are in some way dependent on them; such, for instance, as by comparing the figures for the length, breadth and width of the skull with those for cranial capacities. According to theory we should expect the total range ratio of the last to be approximately the product of the ratios of the other three; and while this is not exactly so, it is sufficiently close to give general support to the theory. Another line of attack which suggests itself is to find a more or less complex trait, some of whose factors may be eliminated from one's calculations by being kept constant, and then noting how the variabilities of the trait, with and without additional factors, compared with one another. Even more crucial would be the experiment of finding some "compound" trait which could be broken up into elements or groups of factors the variabilities of which were known on their own account. According to theory, one would expect that the variability of the compound trait would be approximately equal to the product of the variabilities of its constituent factors. Such an example is furnished by the measurements of vital capacity when age and height are kept constant. This trait when height and age are disregarded has an unusually large total range ratio (3.90); when age is eliminated by restricting our measurement to vital capacities to boys 13 years of age, it becomes 2.75; if stature is now held constant by further restricting our measurement to those of 13 year old boys, 59 inches tall, the total range ratio drops to 2.13. According to our theory, the variability of vital capacity uncontrolled should be equal to the product of the variability of vital capacity with age and height factored out, times the variability of age, times the variability of stature at a given age. We do not know the variability of age per se, but we do know that of height. So let us simplify our problem a bit; namely, compare the variability of vital capacity at a given age with and without stature factored out. The total range ratio for vital capacity for boys 13 years old of all heights is 2.75; for boys 13 years old, 59 inches tall, 2.13; the total range ratio for stature for boys 13 years old is 1.26. Multiplying the variabilities of the second and third items we get 2.68, or approximately that of the variability of the first, which is what we should expect according to our hypothesis: The total range ratio for vital capacity of 13 year old boys of all heights is equal to the product of the total range ratio for vital capacity of 13 year old boys 59 inches tall times the total range ratio for height of 13 year old boys.

The above examples do not of course prove our hypothesis. But while I am not able to furnish more cases, two indirect lines of evidence strongly support it. The first is that whenever one is able to eliminate a group of factors from a given trait or ability, the variability of the measurements of the particular trait is reduced; the second, that relatively "simple" traits usually have much smaller total range ratios than "complex" ones. Thus, the total range ratio for height is less than for body weight, that of speed of running less than that for vital capacity, and so on. And finally, when we come to the "simplest" body capacities like that of body temperature, their variabilities begin to approach those of physical phenomena, from which indeed, they are often hardly distinguishable. One must add, however, that while it is possible to reduce the variability of the measures of human capacity to a considerable degree by eliminating or partialing out perturbing factors, there are even, theoretically, limits to this procedure. The limits are those points beyond which further simplification of the conditions of measurement would alter the character of the trait or ability measured itself.

The reason for this is that the manifestations we call traits and abilities are themselves compound events or resultant phenomena, and we cannot eliminate certain factors without seriously changing or even destroying the phenomena themselves. Whence it follows that even in the case of the simplest traits and abilities we shall be forced to deal with a complex resultant of interacting factors, and accordingly never be able to determine the lower limits of human variability. In the case of the upper limit of human variability, however, the possibility of solution seems more favorable, and several years ago, I thought, though incorrectly, to have successfully demonstrated that its mathematical value was identical with the important logarithmic constant, $e = 2.7182...$ But while this value cannot be said to have been rigorously established, the empirical data at hand shows clearly that this limit is in some way biologically determined by the organic rate of growth, and in any case is not significantly greater in value than the ratio 3.0:1. Thus, of the 73 range ratios given in table 6, just five are greater than 2.718:1, and only two exceed the ratio 3.0:1. Furthermore, the exceptions which are met with occur in those fields of measurement where the complexity of the conditions is such as to make it probable that we are, in these instances, dealing not with single but with peculiarly compounded traits; or again, where the variabilities of the measures is influenced by factors which, in the ordinary sense, cannot be considered germaine constituents of the trait.

A final word as to the hierarchical arrangement of the total range ratios discussed in the last chapter. Our first examination of individual variabilities seemed to suggest that the limits of variability of most human capacities approximated what I termed the *2 to 1 ratio.* This generalization, in the light of accumulated data needs some considerable emendation. It may still be said to be approximately true, if we

TABLE 8

Ratio of the least to the most efficient individual in various gainful occupations (Abridged from Hull)

VOCATION	CRITERIA	RANGE RATIO
Heel trimming—shoes	Number of pairs per day	1.4:1
Loom operation—silk	Per cent of time kept in operation	1.5:1
Hosiery matters	Hourly piecework earning	1.9:1
Loom operation cotton	Earnings	2.0:1
Bottom scoring shoes	Number of pairs per day	2.0:1
Knitting machine operators	Pounds of women's hose per hour	2.2:1
Office boys	Weekly salary	2.3:1
Polishing spoons	Time per 36 spoons	5.1:1
Median		2.0:1

restrict the word capacities to such human performances as are usually included under the term physical and mental abilities. These are the thirty traits and abilities which we have listed under the captions physiological functions (table 19), motor capacities (table 20) and perceptual and mental abilities (table 22). The mean total range ratio for these 30 traits and abilities is 2.25 (median 2.22) with an average deviation[1] (from the

[1] The average rather than the standard deviation is given because of the unsymmetrical distribution of the measures. The S.D. is 0.348, and 90 per cent of the cases are included between the limits 1.80 and 2.79.

mean) of 0.267, or very close to the 2:1 ratio originally suggested. The same may be said of various practical measures of efficiency as, for example, those furnished by a comparison of actual outputs of individuals in different industries. A series of such comparisons taken from *Hull's* book on *Aptitude Testing (40)*, given in table 8, shows that on the average the most efficient individual in any given trade is able to do only about twice as much as the least efficient member of his group.

The 2:1 ratio does not have any general applicability, if we include all human capacities in the wider sense of the term, as defined in chapter II. It then only becomes one of a number of outstanding modes about which the total range ratios of special and generally related types of mental abilities tend to fall. This fact was already indicated when reference was made to the multimodal form of distribution of the total range ratios of the various traits and abilities taken as a whole. Reference again to figure 7, will show that the curve has four distinct peaks, centering about the values 1.20–129, 1.50–1.59, 2.00–2.09 and 2.50–2.59., and all these modes may be looked upon as significant human capacity constants in the same sense as the 2:1 ratio may be said to be worthy of special remark.

The numbers just listed are even more significant in another sense; they bear a remarkable mathematical relation to one another. The numerical value of each succeeding mode is very nearly the successive integral power of the first, taken as a base. Thus, taking the mean of the interval 1.20–1.29, 1.25, or as is more probably correct, 1.26, as the base, the successive values $(1.26)^2$, $(1.26)^3$, $(1.26)^4$ are 1.59, 2.00, 2.52, and these coincide almost exactly with the mean values of the successive modes as actually found. This coincidence cannot be accidental, and we may consider it as further proof of the multiple factor theory of human variability, and, more generally, as evidence for the *dimensional character of human capacities.*

CHAPTER VI

EXCEPTIONS

In going through the tables given in appendix B, the reader will probably have observed that many of the figures recorded for the maximal and minimal values of the traits and abilities listed, were often noticeably inferior to corresponding extremes of individual measurements which he may personally have had occasion to observe, or, at least, to have read of. Indeed, a visit to any good circus or museum of freaks will reveal "giants" measuring considerably in excess of the 6 feet 7 inches which we recorded as the extreme upper limit of human stature, "fat ladies" who tip the scales at more nearly 400 pounds than 250 pounds, as would be expected according to our figures, and "strong" men who can lift weights more nearly ten than two times as heavy as those which the average man can manage. Similar extremes of ability have likewise been noted in the realm of mental abilities, as testified by the feats of "lightning" calculators, the performances of individuals with "phenomenal" memories, and the discoveries of men of genius, to mention the most familiar examples. And of course, greater deviations from the mean than those recorded in our tables, also occur in the opposite directions: midgets considerably less than 4 feet in height, "microcephalics," with crania no larger than a man's fist, and idiots who cannot utter a coherent syllable, let alone repeat five digits.

The occurrence of exceptions of the kind just noted does not in any way invalidate the figures we have given as delimiting the range of human capacities, because by definition we agreed to include within this range only 998 out of every 1000 individuals. This number omits the highest and lowest, one-tenth of 1 per cent of human beings, a proportion which, if we set the total white adult population at approximately 400,000,000 would still leave us some 800,000 persons in our generation alone among whom to look for these exceptional and extraordinary cases. It goes without saying that so large a number is far from a negligible quantity even for several generations, nor do I overlook the fact that the individuals who go to make up these extremes constitute in many ways the most interesting part of humanity, but for reasons already stated, we must omit both geniuses[1] and freaks from our calculations. Nevertheless, I am not unmindful of the fact that these instances cannot entirely be disregarded in any complete discussion of the problem of the range of human capacities. Accordingly, we shall consider some exceptional examples of extraordinary trait and ability records, to see what corrections, if any, they impose on our concepts of human variability. In any case, they will give us some idea as to the glorious heights which the human race can reach, and less encouragingly, of the abysmal deficiencies by which it may be degraded.

We may conveniently begin with examples of extraordinary deviation in the realm of the physical dimensions of man, that have been recorded at diverse times and diverse places. The ancients have handed down to us much lore about their reputed "giants" and "dwarfs," but because of the mythical character of these beings or, at least, lack of scientific verification of their existence, we cannot trust too much to the measurements which they have given us of them. We must therefore bridge many centuries of "history," and rely chiefly upon modern "records," where we have available not only the actual measurements but, in some instances, the skeletal remains of the reputed subjects, which may be rechecked. Of such instances the most frequently cited cases are those of the Irish giant Cornelius McGrath who was 2 m. 63 cm. (7 feet 8 inches) tall, and the unnamed Swedish mammoth in the

[1] The problem of genius and degeneration is discussed in chapter VII.

army of William I of Prussia, who is cited as having measured 8 feet 6 inches. The latter appears to be the tallest actual man in recorded history. At the other extreme, we have more numerous examples, possibly because during the 16th and 17th century dwarfs and midgets were attached as curios at various European courts. The recorded measurements of the smallest of these range from 70 cm. to 90 cm. The most famous one in recent times was the much displayed Tom Thumb (né Charles Stratton) who was exploited by the great American showman Barnum at the end of the last century. Tom is reported to have stood 55 cm. in his stocking feet, and if this is correct enjoys the distinction as the shortest human being who ever attained adulthood.[1]

Anomalies of weight seem to have attracted the interest of collectors of curious facts less often than those of stature, and this may belie the popular belief that everybody likes a fat man. At any rate, statistics about him are less copious. In medical literature there are a number of instances of individuals over 400 pounds, and the greatest I have come across is that cited in Duckworth's System of Medicine[2] of a male, 23 years old, who attained the "incredible weight of 739 pounds." At the other extreme Tom Thumb's weight is given as 17 pounds, and, if accurate, he would seem to hold the all-time record for weight as well as height. For adults who fall within the normal range of stature, 84 pounds is the lowest weight I have come across. This, however, does not include cases of inanition in disease.

Size of individual organs shows high correlation with general body weight and stature, but divergencies are not infrequent,

[1] Among the midgets who have come under my personal observation, I can give the measurements of "Major Mite." The "major," when I saw him (December, 1932) was 34 inches tall and weighed 27½ pounds. He was then, or claimed to be, 22 years old. On the Binet intelligence tests he made a mental age score of 9 years 4 months. Both his parents, as well as the other members of his family were of normal stature.

[2] By C. P. Howard and E. S. Mills, article on Obesity (23).

although generally associated with pathological conditions. With disease nearly every organ of the body may become atrophied or hypertrophied, and it is often very difficult to decide whether the atypical cases ought to be included as extremes in the normal variation of the organ or be discarded as instances of pathological manifestations. The question is further complicated by the fact that the viscera and excised organs available for statistical analysis are generally derived from deceased hospital patients which are of course selected populations. Finally, there is the fact that some of the organs are of a vestigial character (e.g., the spleen), and the extreme variabilities met among them cannot be properly evaluated. The size and weight of the brain, however, and, to a lesser degree, the heart, in spite of their liability to disease, are relatively free from these influences, and the recorded extreme variabilities of these organs may be accepted with greater confidence.

Possibly because of the suspected correlation between size of the brain and intelligence, the human encephalon and its subadjoining parts have been the object of much systematic measurement. All investigations agree that, compared with that of other organs, as well as the body as a whole, the variability of the normal brain is relatively small. The mean weights of the male and female cerebrum are approximately 1400 and 1300 grams respectively, with the corresponding "normal" extremes in the vicinity of 1750 and 1100 grams for males, and 1600 and 900 for females (Retzius' Swedish data).[1] But in the case of the condition known as an encephally (of course, partial) the weight of the brain may be greatly diminished, and many cases are reported in medical literature of weights under 500 grams. In this connection it must be noted that most of the weights recorded are of microcephalics who

[1] Pearl (70). Nevertheless Wilder (104) reported the case of an otherwise normal man (5 feet 1 inch, 148 pounds, and not mentally defective, with a brain weighing only 680 grams.

died before maturity (age 21), but as the size of the brain attains its maximum relatively early (between the ages of 10 and 15), the comparisons of even young microcephalics with the adult brain do not introduce much source of error, providing, of course, they would have attained the minimum age indicated. In any case, there are quite a number of brain weights of adult microcephalics, reported in medical literature, below 500 grams, the lowest on record being that of an Italian female, age 41, with a brain weighing only 289 grams. The woman was naturally a mental defective, but above the grade of idiot.

Very large[1] brains, unlike very small ones, do not seem to be associated with pathological conditions. The maximum weight reported for the human brain is in the vicinity of 2000 grams. The brain of Cromwell is said to have weighed 2231 grams, that of Byron, 2200, but neurologists (Spitzka) are inclined to reject figures for these two as unreliable. On the other hand, the reported weight of Turgenieff's brain (2015 grams) which was also at first questioned is now accepted and appears to be the undisputed maximum on record.[2]

The dimensions which we have included under the term

[1] That is, of course, heavy ones. The "large" brain of the hydrocephalic is not so much gravid, as distended.

[2] It is to be noted that the "heavy" brains reported have usually been those of men of genius, and there would seem to be some correlation, though not a great one, between size of brain and mental capacity. The evidence is not based upon systematic computation of correlation ratios, but is indirectly inferred from such facts, that comparisons between the mean weights of the brains of "men of achievement" and those of the general population, show that the former exceed those of the latter by approximately 100 grams. Nevertheless, some men of unusual ability have had unusually small brains, as for instance those of Gambetta (1294 grams) and Gall (1194 grams); the brain of Walt Whitman weighed only 1182 grams, or more than 200 grams less than that of the average male adult. What seems to be the explanation here, as in the case of most other traits, is that a certain minimum is required for effectiveness of function, but that possession of an amount above this minimum is not necessarily associated with superiority of an ability dependent upon the functioning of the organ involved.

metabolic and physiologic constants are at once among the least and most variable, depending on whether or not pathological cases are excluded. Under normal conditions, the total range ratios for these capacities are in the vicinity of 1.5:1 and 2.0:1, the smallest variabilities found being those of body temperature and the chemical constituents and properties of the blood, including its hydrogen ion concentration (1.35:1). But in case of disease and special pathological conditions maximal and minimal values of both metabolic and physiologic capacities, particularly the latter, may deviate widely from their normal limits. In some instances however, the variability even in disease is small, and of these the two least variable again are body temperature and the hydrogen ion concentration of the blood.

The temperature of the body which under normal conditions varies within the approximate limits of 97.5 to 99.5, may fluctuate at most by only a few degrees in either direction. In the case of fever it may rise as much as 6 or 7 degrees, but temperatures of 106°F. (in adults) are usually fatal. Nevertheless temperatures as high as 108 and 109°F. have been reported, and Krehl (49) states that in heat-stroke they may reach as high as 110°F., and over.[1] Figures for subnormal temperatures show even less wide deviation from the mean. In case of shock and certain brain tumors, the body temperatures, may drop 2 or 3°F., but temperatures below 94°F. are extremely rare though not unrecorded. Dr. N. E. Selby of the Neurological Institute informs me that there was recently a patient on the wards of the Montefiore Hospital (New York) with a pituitary tumor, who for weeks ran a temperature between 90 and 92°F., and that is about the lowest on record.

The hydrogen ion concentration of the blood like body temperature also exhibits but small range of variation even in disease. The normal range in health is from pH –7.3 to

[1] If so, they are immediately followed by death.

pH –7.5 (Van Slyke, 96), but any considerable degree of hyper- or hypoacidity is very soon fatal. According to Van Slyke (96), human life is not possible when the blood reaches a pH of less than –7.0 or more than –7.9, and the figures of some more recent investigators show even a smaller range, particularly for the upper limit.[1] On the other hand there are a few instances of metabolic and physiologic "constants" which, while showing a restricted range in health, may show very great fluctuations in disease. Among the more outstanding are the number of red and white cells in the blood, the former of which while not fluctuating far from a mean of 5,000,000 per centimeter in health, may run as high as 15,000,000 (Harrap, 33) in cases of polycythemia, and considerably below 1,000,000 in pernicious anemia (Cornell, 16).[2] In leukemia the mean number of 8,000 white corpuscles per cubic centimeter of blood in the average healthy person may be increased to over 1,000,000 (McRae, 58).

Intermediate as regards increased variability under the influence of disease are the fluctuations of the heart and respiratory rate. The human heart (adults) which is normally geared to a rate of from 60 to 80 beats per minute will under certain conditions (paroxysmal tachycardia) surpass 200, and if counted in terms of auricular contractions may be even as high as 340, as in heart "flutter" (Lewis, 53a). At the other

[1] The restricted limits of blood acidity, within which life is possible are very strikingly shown by the ion equivalents of the pH figures. A pH of –7.0 signifies that there is one negatively charged ion in every 10,000,000 hydrogen atoms, a pH of –7.6 a concentration of one negatively charged ion to approximately every 40,000,000 atoms. Taking pH –7.0 and pH –7.6 as the limits of human blood acid tolerance, simple calculation $\left(\text{the difference between } \frac{1}{10{,}000{,}000} - \frac{1}{40{,}000{,}000}\right)$ shows that the addition or subtraction of one ion to approximately every 13,000,000 atoms is all that is necessary to upset the physico-chemical balance we call life.

[2] In a recent number of the American Journal of Science, Kastlin (46), reported a case of Agranulitic Angina with an astounding blood count of only 100 red cells.

extreme, in heart block, the rate may drop to as low as 16 beats per minute. Hardly less marked are the pathological deviations of the respiratory rate. The normal upper limit of 20 per minute may be increased to as much as 80 or 90 in heart failure,[1] in pernicious anemia and in certain types of encephalitis. On the other hand, in morphine poisoning, in trance and cataleptic stupor, the rate has been known to drop to as low as 3 or 4 times per minute. Finally, blood pressure (systolic) while not showing such wide fluctuations as either the pulse or heart rate, can on occasion surpass the normal limits by considerable amounts, particularly at the upper extreme (e.g., 300 mm. Hg in marked essential hypertension). In Addison's disease, it may fall as low as 60 or even 40, but these are usually predeath occurrences. Bloodpressures below 75, unless temporary, are usually fatal.[2]

Leaving the field of the simpler physical and physiological dimensions of the body and its diverse organs, and turning to the complex capacities dependent upon them, one finds even more striking divergences as regards the maximal and minimal values we have accorded them in our tables, but their evaluation is also more dubious. Direct comparisons of unusual feats of strength, for example, or of physical endurance, speed of movement, with performances of the average person are, to begin with, much more difficult, because such feats have usually been performed by practised or specially trained individuals, and we do not know what the capacities of the average individual would be in these fields, if similarly trained. Again, while history abounds with examples of men of gigantic strength and superhuman endurance, it is not always possible to separate fact from fancy. This of course holds particularly for the feats related by the ancients. The testimony offered

[1] Rates of 50 and more are relatively common in pneumonia and heart failure.

[2] I am indebted for some of these facts to Dr. Norman Jolliffe, Associate in Medicine, Psychiatric Division, Bellevue Hospital, New York City.

to us by the chroniclers of the Middle Ages are somewhat better documented, but the stories of the extraordinary demonstrations of physical strength and agility, called forth by the tournaments and the fields of personal combat of feudal times, though undoubtedly based on fact, likewise cannot very well be authenticated. Nevertheless, even though we neglect these two rich sources, and restrict ourselves to the substantiated feats recorded in recent times, enough of the extraordinary remains to arouse our wonderment. Mere enumeration of them would fill many pages, and I must refer the interested reader to the diverse books on sport records and the like which are concerned with them. The following are some of the more outstanding examples.

Henry Sullivan who was the second man to swim the English Channel (1923) was in the water for 27 consecutive hours during which time he covered 45 miles; five years later (1928) Otto Kemmerich swam the Bay of Danzig, a distance of 55 miles, in 43 hours. In 1888 G. Littlewood (New York) ran 100 miles in a little over 13 hours, without stopping, and in a six day race (England 1882) one contestant ran 531 miles in 144 hours. These are seemingly among the greatest feats of physical endurance in recent times. A close second are some of the long prize fights before the days of the Queensbury rules. Thus in 1789, one Jonathan Smith is reported to have fought a James Kelley with bare knuckles and without interruption for 6½ hours, and in 1825 Jack Jones contended with Patsy Tunney for 376 rounds, the fight lasting 4½ hours. For sheer strength, there are instances of such feats as tearing a two inch telephone book in two, and pulling a loaded automobile truck with one's teeth, feats which perhaps also involve some special knacks, but H. Lansing of Cincinnati, O. in a weight lifting contest raised 1384 pounds unaided (1888) and A. Corcoran (Chicago, 1873) lifted a 12 pound dumb-bell 1400 times before making a halt. In the matter of mere speed the discrepancies between the average and the "fastest" human are not so great, but with each holding of Olympic games new records are being added. At the present, among the most imposing ones are the time records for the 100 meter (9.6 seconds), 1 mile (4 minutes 8 seconds) and 10,000 meter races (30 minutes 18.8 seconds), held by Metcalfe (1932), Lovelock (1933) and Pavo Nurmi (1928), respectively.[1]

When we come to instances of mental prowess, the feats recorded are at once both more impressive and more difficult to evaluate. This difficulty is in part due to the fact that many of our mental abilities, as already pointed out (chapter II), do not lend themselves to direct measurement, and in part to the fact that our quantitative estimates of them, such as they are, are further complicated by social evaluations. On this latter point, as well as on the question of the interpretation of qualitative differences, I shall have more to say later on, but as our interest for the time being is primarily in "facts and figures," I shall for the present confine my citations of exceptional performances in the mental sphere to those of such capacities and abilities as have actually furnished us with quantitatively comparable data.

The least disputed examples of exceptional mental ability are in the realm of simple retention and recall (rote memory). The auditory rote memory of the average adult is 7 digits, and the upper limit of normality 10 to 11, or a little over twice the number at the other end of normality. Persons with memory spans of from 12 to 15 digits are not so infrequent as to be classed as rarities, but individuals who can reproduce as many as 20 digits are decidedly so. Yet Binet in his study of lightning calculators found that one of them, Inaudi, had the almost unbelievable capacity of repeating 42 digits immediately after presentation without an error either as to number or position.

Reports of feats of memory depending upon associative learning and the ability to reproduce quantities of material after long intervals are no less impressive, though less easily

[1] These and the foregoing items are taken from the World Almanacs for 1910, 1913 and 1929 (103). Lovelock's record is from newspaper reports.

expressed as multiples of the capacities of the average individual along similar lines. Particularly outstanding again are the feats of lightning calculators whose phenomenal memories are very often, though not exclusively, confined to the retention of numbers involved in their calculations. Such, for example, was the case of the boy prodigy, Alex Guin, who at the age of 8 knew the logarithms of the numbers 1 to 1000 by heart; and the great Gauss is said to have been able to give at once "the first decimals of all the logarithms." The mathematician, George Wallis, telling of his facile memory narrates that on one occasion he amused himself by extracting mentally the square root of a number containing 53 digits, and a month later reproducing both the number and root correctly. And it is told of the great Euler that, suffering one night from insomnia, he attempted to assuage his sleeplessness by calculating the sixth powers of each of the natural numbers from one to twenty. These he reproduced a few days later to a class of students.[1]

While the memory feats of lightning calculators and mathematicians are among the most spectacular they are matched by no less astounding performances of other gifted individuals, literary figures, artists, scholars, and even some who otherwise have no special claim to eminence. Beginning with unsung students who have been known to memorize whole chapters or even an entire volume when "cramming" for an examination, secretaries who after listening for an hour or more to an address have been able to reproduce it later without missing a word, and musicians who know entire symphonies and operas by heart, we come to the almost unbelievable memories of a Pascal, Macaulay and the great Gaon of Wilna, the last of whom is said to have known by heart both the Babylonian and Jerusalem Talmud.[2] But even more remarkable, though less impressive to the common eye, because less understood,

[1] These items are culled from the Articles of Scripture (84) and Mitchel (63) on mathematical prodigies.

[2] A total of about 40 volumes.

are the discoveries and speculations of the great scientists,—the experiments of a Faraday, the deductions of a Newton, the theories of an Einstein. In their achievements we have another type of exception, the exception that consists of an ability to perceive new facts and new relations, that is, relations which however obvious or easy to master *after* they have been discovered, are nevertheless imperceptible to the mass of mankind *before* their discovery. This ability to perceive new relationships is in itself a special ability and one that seemingly differs from most others by what looks like an all or non characteristic. This seeming all or non quality of the ability, has led some to suppose that "it is something which you either have or haven't." This conclusion is not warranted; it is not the ability which one either has or hasn't, but the perception of the new relationship in question in any given case, that is the new *Gestalt*. One either sees or doesn't see a particular configuration,[1] and, in this sense, the perception of a Gestalt is an all or none phenomenon; but different individuals are able to see varying numbers of configurations in the same set of data; in this sense, the ability to perceive relationships is a capacity that varies like any other of our abilities. Nevertheless, it must be admitted that the ability to perceive new relationships lends itself but little to precise measurement. Often too, it seems less remarkable than it in fact is, because unlike the extremes of achievement in other types of ability, it seemingly lacks the character of inimitability.[2] If a person cannot repeat 20 digits, no amount of

[1] That is due to the fact that a Gestalt is not a function of its parts, but its totality. You cannot partly see a Gestalt, because any part of a configuration is itself a configuration, that is a different Gestalt.

[2] As an example, consider Newton's great discovery of the law of gravitation. This discovery was not the consequence of a sudden inspiration occasioned by the fall of an apple, as popular legend would have it, but the result of a systematic application of Galileo's law of falling bodies and Kepler's laws of planetary motions to Tycho Brahe's astronomical tables. Off hand, the consequent enunciation of the law would accordingly seem like an inevitable mathematical induction from the facts at hand. In one sense this

listening to one who can will enable him to do so; but even a person of average mathematical ability may be able to repeat the proof of the law of inverse squares. In spite of this fact, however, the ability to perceive new relationships is one of the rarest of all gifts, and the one upon which more than any other of our abilities the human race owes its greatest achievements.

---

is so. Furthermore the mathematical reasoning is not much more difficult than that of an ordinary proposition in analytics, and considerably less complicated than that of many problems which college students are asked to solve. What then is so remarkable about Newton's discovery? It is this,—that Newton was able to discern a relation which, when exposed, becomes so patent as to make one wonder why it was not obvious to others, but whose perception required such stroke of genius, that even the great Kepler with practically the same facts before him was unable to see it. It remained for Newton to see the next step. Nearly all great discoveries seem to have consisted in just this, that their authors were able to see this "next step."

CHAPTER VII

THE BURDEN OF AGE

One of the self evident facts about human capacities is that they do not remain stationary. Most apparent, of course, are the changes observed in early life, which in their entirety are summed up by the word growth. They begin, as we know, with birth, and continue in a more or less striking manner to that ill-defined period we call adulthood. With this obvious fact we shall not be concerned. The questions which I wish to discuss here, are the variability in rate at which growth takes place, the question as to the age or ages at which mental and physical growth may be said to terminate, and most fully of all, the relation of age to physical and intellectual virility in man.

To the first of these questions, anthropometrists and psychologists have devoted considerable effort, and the results of their investigations may be easily summarized: Growth, both physical and mental is very rapid in the first years of life, becomes decreasingly less as the child grows older, and as adulthood is approached the yearly increments become smaller and smaller until they entirely vanish. The rate of growth even for short periods, as can be seen from the curves shown on page 83, is not uniform. Nor is the rate of growth the same for different traits, though there is a tendency for many of the growth curves to resemble the one shown in figure 8 which is often referred to as the "typical" curve of growth. But different curves of growth often deviate from it both as to general form and special peculiarities. For example, the alterations in weight of the brain from birth to maturity are relatively small as compared with the changes in the weight of the body as a whole; vision and hearing attain their maximum efficiency quite early in life (before 15) whereas vital capacity and strength of grip comparatively late (about 30).

The growth of mental abilities, in so far as we are able to measure them accurately, seems to conform in general to the typical curve of growth pictured above, except that certain mental functions may show special periods of rapid improvement or relative stagnation. For instance, retentiveness, after showing marked improvement in infancy and early childhood,

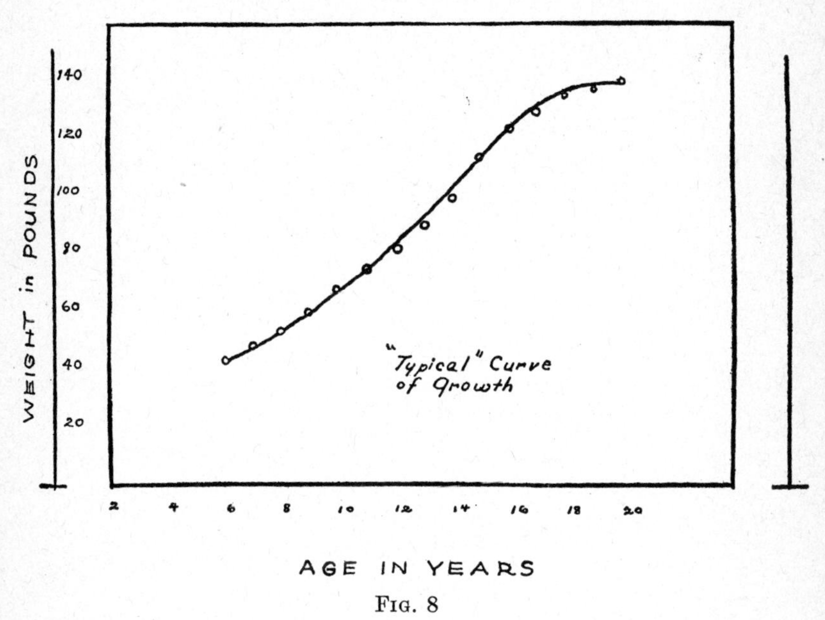

FIG. 8

seems to hit a plateau between the ages of 10 and 13; rapid alterations in reasoning ability are less apparent, and its development appears more continuous. It is, however, altogether possible that this observation is an artifact due to our uncertain and limited means of measuring mental abilities.[1]

[1] The actual form of the growth curve of general intelligence is still in dispute, but variations of form noted seem to depend primarily upon the type of unit of measurement employed in plotting the curve. Professor Thurstone (95), for example has shown that the growth curve of intelligence may be

The occurrence of plateaux, or periods of apparent stagnation in growth curves of certain mental functions, also brings up the question as to whether, in the measurement of mental capacities, we may not be dealing with what in mathematics and physics are known as discontinuous functions, that is, quantities which increase (or decrease) by sudden leaps. Continuous functions, on the contrary, are such whose quantities vary without any gaps, that is, must pass through all intermediate points before attaining any given value. All physical capacities seem to be such functions.[1] Thus, before a man has attained the weight of 157 pounds he must have first weighed 156 pounds, 155 pounds, etc. But this does not seemingly hold in all processes. Thus, in case of sudden solutions which "flash through the mind," one seems to jump from complete bafflement to complete insight. Professor Köhler (48) indeed thinks that this method of discovery is primary to all learning. But it is, of course, also possible that this

---

markedly altered by the simple process of transmuting test scores from one to another system of units. He insists that the plotting of a true curve of growth requires a previous determination of an absolute zero point of ability. He himself defines the absolute zero point of general intelligence as "the mean test performance at which variability vanishes," and having determined the point mathematically, uses the standard deviation of a favored age group (year 17), as the absolute unit of measurement. I do not myself believe that this method necessarily gives us the "true curve of growth," but it is of interest because it severely challenges some of the time honored conclusions regarding its supposed "laws." For example, contrary to what we have just concluded, intelligence does not augment in early years by decreasing increments, but shows "a positive acceleration up to the general age level of about ten years." This means that intelligence increases less per year at lower age levels (e.g., at age 3) than at higher level in childhood (e.g., at year 9), a fact which Professor Thurstone's curve of growth shows undeniably. I believe, however, that the form of curve which he obtained, is contingent upon the type of material with which he measured intelligence, namely the linguistic and scholastic character of the Binet tests. Moreover, I do not esteem the standard deviation a "truer unit of measurement" than some others that have been used. The arguments against the assumption that it is, have already been advanced (chapter II). See also appendix A.

[1] In the light of the latest theories regarding the structure of the atom this is not strictly true.

discontinuity is only apparent, and merely indicates our inability to measure or even detect intermediate steps.

But to return to our main problem: What is the relation of age to physical and mental virility? To be able to answer this question completely we should have to have systematic data on a great many individuals, with respect to their various abilities at successive periods of their life. The measurements would have to be strictly comparable and comprehend the entire span of human life. Unfortunately, except for statistics on body, weight and stature, we are far from having these data. Most studies on the influence of age only cover the period from early childhood up to adulthood, that is, from approximately the age of 5 to 16 or 17.[1] Individuals over 18 have usually been studied as a single group, namely, as adults. Noteworthy exceptions, however, have been the researches emanating from Professor Pearson's laboratory, particularly those of Ruger (81a), Elderton (24) and a few others who have worked up the data collected by Galton in England almost a half century ago, and the studies of Jones (43, 44) and Miles (61, 62) in this country on general intelligence, which, on the contrary, are of quite recent date. Numerically, the individuals who acted as subjects in the observations made by Galton still constitute the most extensive age groups thus far studied with respect to any considerable number of traits and capacities. The available data cover measurements made on some 11,000 men, women and children from the ages of 5 to 80 with respect to the following traits: stature, sitting height, span, body weight, strength of pull, grip of right, left and stronger hands, swiftness of blow, vital capacity, visual acuity, highest audible pitch, sense of perpendicularity, and errors of bisection and trisection. Below the ages of 9 and above the ages of 70 the number of individuals measured was generally too small for reliable statistical analysis, but this

[1] The recent work on infants and the study of pre-school children have partly remedied the defect at the lower end of the age curve.

deficiency will not interfere with the general valuation of the data, because both are clearly beyond the points either of maximum virility or initial decline.

The curves of growth and decline for the capacities just enumerated (examples given in figs. 9A to 9C) have been carefully worked up by Ruger and Stoesinger (81a), and Elderton and Moul (24), and I shall briefly summarize their findings, using one of their typical curves as a paradigm. Inspection of this curve (fig. 9A) which, with the exception of the linear traits, is typical for most of the other capacities studied, shows that in its initial portion, i.e., up to the age of 20, its general characteristics are identical with those of the typical curve of growth, to wit, rapid rise in the first years with a gradual slackening as adulthood is approached, except that at puberty, there is a short period of acceleration giving rise to what is known as the pubescent hump. All this is familiar. The new facts are those which are reached by the age curve after the 18th or 20th year. These are: first, that growth or improvement in capacity, while not yet entirely completed, continues only for a comparatively short time thereafter, i.e., until about the age of 24 or 25 where it seemingly attains its maximum. Second, that once it has attained its maximum it does not, as is commonly supposed, remain stationary, but forthwith begins to decline. The decline is at first imperceptible; in the case of static traits like stature it is negligible until about the age of 40, is more marked after middle age is passed, and becomes very conspicuous as old age is approached. For motor functions like swiftness of blow, etc., the characteristics are very much the same as those of static traits up to adulthood, but the decline begins earlier, and that of old age is much more marked. The cases of other functions like strength of pull, vital capacity, etc., are very similar, as are also those of perceptual abilities, when due allowance is made for the manner in which the traits are measured.

Galton's investigations did not include any growth studies

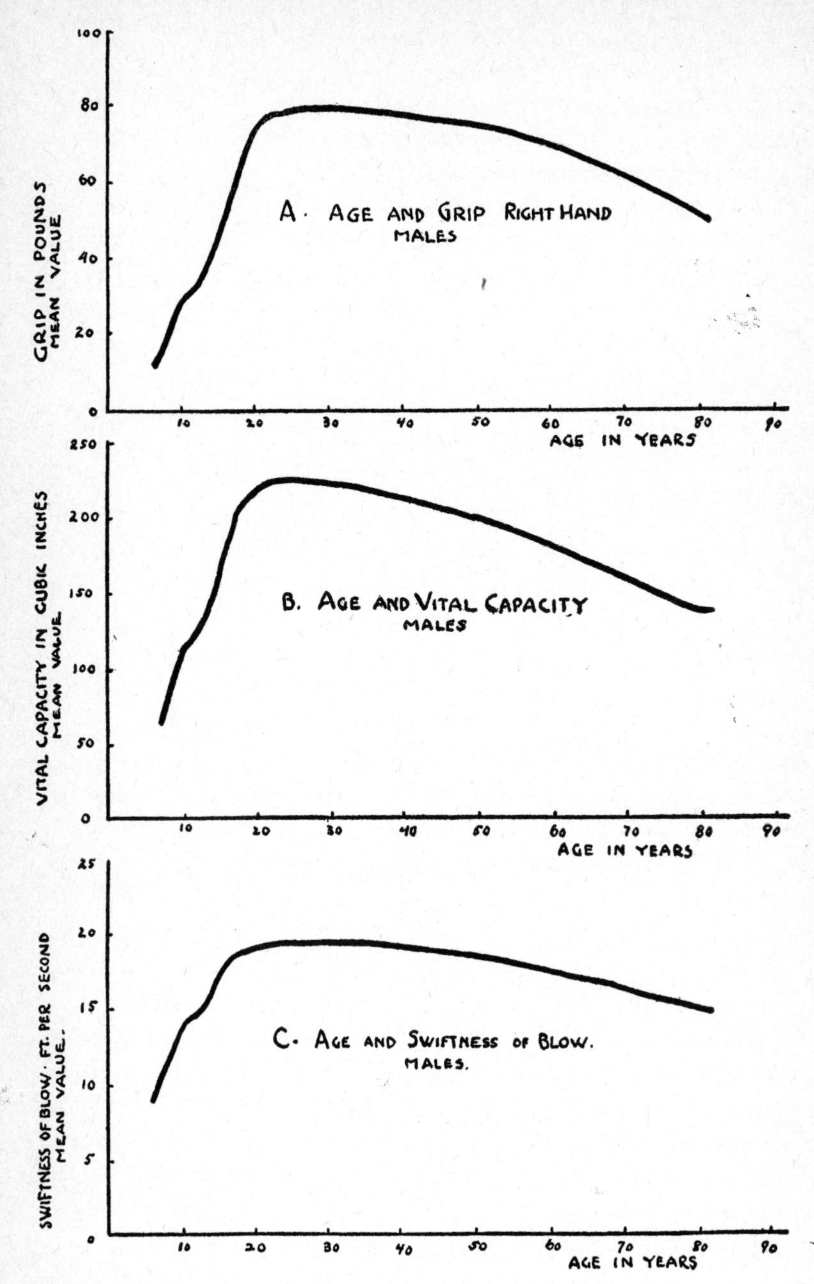

FIGS. 9A, 9B AND 9C. CURVES OF GROWTH FOR FULL SPAN OF LIFE
(Galton's data. Adapted from Ruger and Stoessiger)

of intellectual abilities, and similar curves of growth did not exist for these functions until very recently, in spite of the huge amount of mental testing that was done during the last two decades. Two exceptions, or at least part exceptions, were certain of the data resulting from the Army Alpha Intelligence Examination of soldiers, and the very interesting and more familiar study of Jones who examined the entire popu-

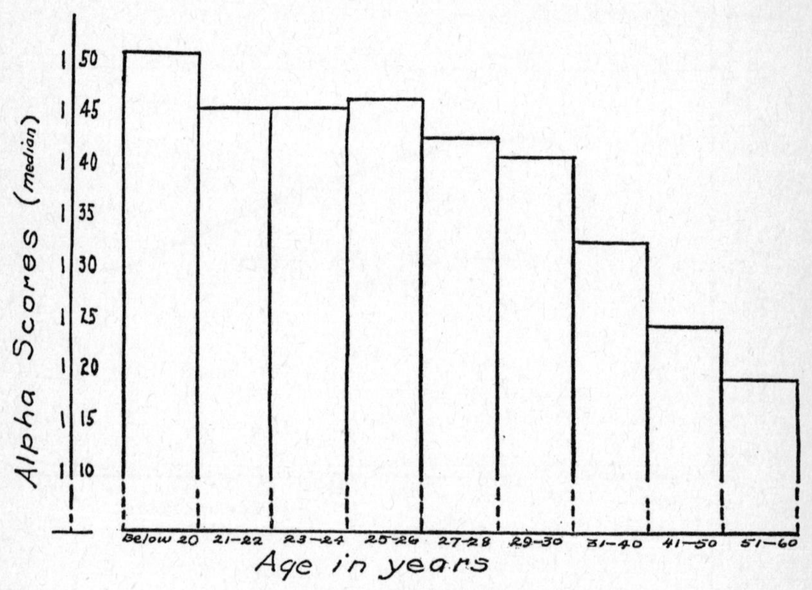

FIG. 10. AGE AND INTELLIGENCE SCORES
(15,385 Officers, U. S. A. Army)

lation of a New England village. The results of the Army examination of some fifteen thousand white officers are summarized by the histogram shown in figure 10. As can be seen at once, it shows that intelligence scores begin to fall off at the age of 20; that after a short plateau, they decline slowly but steadily; and that beginning at the age of about 35, their decline is increasingly marked. The data of Jones, to the extent to which they cover the same age groups, furnish almost identical results. The age-span covered by them is greater, but still insufficient to furnish us with a life curve like those available to us from Galton's data. This lack, however, has recently been filled by the excellent studies of Miles who examined several thousand subjects, ages 12 to 80, with the Otis Intelligence Tests. The results he obtained with these tests now enable us to arrive at an intelligence growth curve that may be compared with those available for physical abilities. I have made such comparison by plotting a growth curve from

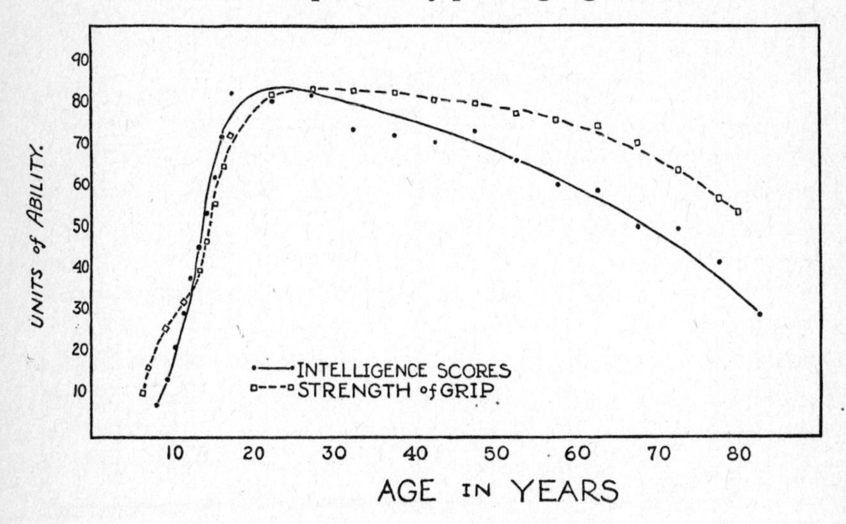

FIG. 11. DECLINE OF PHYSICAL AND MENTAL ABILITY WITH AGE
(For interpretation see text)

the Miles mean intelligence scores at different age levels, and superimposed it on one of the typical life curves obtained by Ruger and Stoessinger from Galton's data (that for strength of grip). These two curves, drawn to approximately the same scale, are shown in figure 11, that for general intelligence being the one represented by the unbroken line.

Examination of the "intelligence" growth curve just mentioned shows that it differs but little in its general aspects from the typical growth curves of physical, physiological and psychomotor abilities. Only, contrary to popular anticipation, the point of optimal achievement in the case of intelligence occurs rather earlier than it does in the case of at least a large number of physical and physiological capacities. There is still some growth in intelligence after fifteen which is now generally accepted as the approximate age at which the intellectual capacities cease to grow; but what is even more striking than this is that after twenty-five (or at most thirty) our intellectual capacities are definitely on the decline, and, just as in the case of physical strength, continue to fall off progressively with age.

If the fact that intellectual growth stops at about the age of fifteen has been a hard fact to accept, the indication that intelligence after attaining its maximum forthwith begins to decline just as any other physiological capacity, instead of maintaining itself at its highest level over a long period of time, has been an even more bitter pill to swallow. It has, in fact, proved so unpalatable that psychologists have generally chosen to avoid noticing it. Thus, though one of the few unequivocally demonstrated facts revealed by the statistical analysis of the intelligence tests data obtained from the examination of the American army was the continuous decrease of test scores with increasing age, the authors of this article, in no way hesitant in drawing less cogent inferences at other points of their discussion, content themselves here with the conclusion that the results "cannot be said, on the present information to point to a lowering of intelligence with age." Yet, as Professor Spearman (85) has well pointed out, no reason is given "as to how this conclusion may be avoided." The fact is that, on the basis of these data (as an examination of the tables will testify), it cannot. Nor do I believe that it can on any other available data, although some of them indicate that it *might* be. Thus Hollingworth (37), testing some five hundred adults with a battery of four tests, found that only on one of them did the older men do conspicuously more poorly. On two of the tests the younger and older did about equally well, and on one the younger performed slightly less well. But with regards to these data, it might first be pointed out that Hollingworth's age groups did not go beyond 45 (the age beyond which mental decline begins to be conspicuous) and secondly, that on the one test which showed a significant change, it was in the direction of a falling off of ability with increasing age. Two other studies (cited by Professor Spearman) which seemingly give solace to those who hold the view that mental abilities remain unimpaired until advanced age, are the investigations of Beeson (5) and the study of Taylor and Foster (27). The first of these may be discredited altogether, not only because the number of individuals tested was small, only ten men and ten women, but because the subjects were a very selected group. The second study cited, far from offering such solace, turns out, on actual examination, to be a veritable refutation of the very view which it had been called in to support. Chiefly on the basis of the data furnished by Taylor and Foster, Professor Spearman concludes that general intelligence, or more precisely its principal factor "g," after attaining its highest point "retains its maximum level unaltered right up to the end of life (or at least to the onset of senility),"[1] because in a great majority of the tests the oldest subjects showed no failure whatsoever. But after carefully reviewing the cited study of Foster and Taylor I find not the slightest basis for this assertion. On the contrary the authors in their original article after summarizing their data specifically state that, "with advancing age there is a tendency for scores in each test to fall off." The tendency is most marked in the case of memory and the more difficult tests (dissected sentences, naming words in three minutes) and "least marked . . . in the very easy tests" (comparison of lines, comparison of weights, etc.). The authors were very careful about drawing any broad inferences from their data, because, as they specifically

[1] Loc. cit., p. 375.

mention, some of their groups were not strictly comparable.[1] Indeed their main interest in study seems to have been to discover the type of test on which older subjects do better or less well than younger ones. "The main conclusion," adduce the authors, "to be drawn from our work thus far is that, whether we study normal or psychotic persons with the *same total score*,[2] the younger persons tend to excel in giving words in three minutes, in building sentences and drawing from memory, while the older excel in detecting absurdities and in defining in abstract terms." The question of the relative intellectual levels of the younger and older subjects did not come here at all under consideration, since the groups compared had previously been equated with respect to these very items, i.e.; their general intelligence ratings. Apparently Professor Spearman entirely overlooked the phrase "with the same total score," an oversight which is particularly hard to explain in an otherwise so careful researcher. Nor can one easily explain why, in coming to his own general conclusions, he should have disregarded so completely the results of the Army Alpha examinations, after having previously recognized their importance, unless we assume some unconscious bias. I am myself inclined to ascribe these "oversights" to the unpleasantness of the impending conclusion, and to the even less palatable corollaries which the acceptance of this conclusion carries with it These corollaries I shall presently consider in some detail, but before doing so, I wish to dispose of yet another line of "evidence" which has been put forth as "proof" of the fact that individuals maintain their intellectual virility at approximately its maximum level right up to the end of their natural life. I refer to various genetic and statistical studies of genius, particularly those that involve estimation of age of maximal virility from dates of publications of greatest works

[1] The age group 20 to 29 years, for example being described as "distinctly inferior in social status."

[2] Italics mine.

or ages at which men of eminence and genius have supposedly made their greatest contribution.

We may begin by calling attention to the fact that the statistical study of men of genius and their achievements is subject to various difficulties and pitfalls which make inferences based upon them far from incontrovertible. There are, to start with, the difficulties of selection: First, there is the question of the validity of any investigator's choice of the individuals included in his list of men of eminence; second, the individuals being admitted, of the legitimacy of his particular choices of what are or are not to be counted as their *magnum opus*. The selections when made by a single judge are always influenced by personal bias or individual preference, and as such are subject to large errors of judgment. In this respect, some of the earlier and also some of the more recent writers on the subject (e.g., Dorland) are open to much criticism. Since Galton showed the way, however, attempts have been made to reduce this source of error, either by basing selections on composite ratings of several judges, or by arriving at them independently through statistical analysis of biographical compendia of various sorts. Thus, in some of his studies, Thorndike[1] chose his subjects partly on the basis of the amount of space given them in the Dictionary of National Biography and in the Encyclopedia Britannica, the general theory being that in the long run, the space given an individual would be proportionate to his historical importance. This might, at first thought, seem to be a very flimsy procedure, since what it does is simply to shift the onus of choice to some unknown person (the author of the article), and makes it dependent upon the bias or verbosity of the individual who happened to have been assigned to the task of writing the biographical sketch.[2] The stricture cannot be entirely dismissed, but is in

[1] Adult Intelligence (91), p. 303. See also Galton (28) and Cattell (11).

[2] Or perhaps literary ability of the biographer. Thus Johnson owes the large amount of space alloted to him in the Britannica to the fact that his biographical sketch was written by Macaulay.

part to be discounted by the fact that the choice of individuals is supposedly based on established historical evaluation, and in part by the fact that personal idiocyncracies have been more or less compensated for, by the use of not one, but several encyclopedia. In any case it would be difficult to replace this procedure with a less arbitary one.[1]

A much more serious source of error is the localization of the age or moment of greatest mental virility of one's subjects, however chosen. In the case of statesmen and men of affairs, for example, the periods at which they exerted greatest authority, the epochs at which they were able to carry through their most important projects or received their greatest honors, and hence the moments at which they have generally been judged as having attained the zenith of their careers, will only seldom correspond to the years of their greatest intellectual virility. Nevertheless, most writers on the subject have fallen into the error of identifying the two. Thus Dorland (23a) takes 1801 as the year which marked the zenith of Jefferson's intellectual virility (when Jefferson was 58), seemingly, for the mere reason that it coincided with the date of his ascendency to the presidency. But while the presidency is the supreme American symbol of social recognition, nothing that Jefferson did during that year or in the remaining years of his tenure compares in brilliance with his drafting of the Declaration of Independence, achieved at the age of 33. So also does this author take the years of Disraeli's premiership as the period of the great statesman's intellectual zenith, forgetting that owing to political, social and other circumstances, Disraeli had to wait nearly 30 years for the opportunity of exercising the abilities which he had already displayed more than two decades before.

In the case of men of science, much error results from the easy habit of identifying the acme of a man's intellectual powers with the date of publication of his *magnum opus*. A

[1] For justifications of the method see Cattell, loc. cit.

good example is here furnished again by Dorland who places Copernicus' age of maximal intellectual virility at 75, the year in which was published his *De Revolutionibus Orbium Coelestium.* This assumption, however, is certainly not justified. In the first place, the date of publication of the De Revolutionibus does not even remotely coincide with the epoch of its completion. Actually it was finished many years before, and had been kept under cover by Copernicus for 13 years, because of his fear of persecution by the Church. Secondly, and more seriously perhaps, to accept the date of publication of the book as coincident with the period of the author's greatest fertility, would be to disregard almost entirely the long years which he labored over the opus before its completion. We now know that Copernicus came to the belief of the heliocentric theory of the universe long before he announced his "discovery."

The foregoing instances illustrate the inevitable error to which the identification of social recognition or political ascendency with ages of greatest intellectual power will generally lead. In most cases such identification will advance the posited age of the individual's intellectual zenith by a greater or lesser number of years. Either through custom or established practice, positions of importance and authority have nearly always been reserved for older men, and often definitely closed to younger ones. Thus, by law, no man may become president of the United States before he is 36, and where there is no legal limitation the established order generally requires the individual to pursue a graduated ascent of political stepping stones before giving him access to the higher places. By that time he is usually well beyond middle age.

It is only in the case of social upheavals, where trust and power fall into hands of those who are best able to wield it, or in the case of accidents of royal birth, where the individual is endowed with special privileges, that youth finds no bar to opportunity. Thus it is that the French Revolution brings forth Robespierres and Napoleons and not Clemenceaus and

Joffres. The case of military leadership is particularly instructive. In times of peace seniority and politics are largely the basis for advancement, so that in the beginning of a war at least, it is the older men who lead the armies, but in the free for all during times of upheaval, or when special circumstances intervene, as for instance, the accident of royal birth, youth has a chance to come to the fore. At any rate, it cannot be by pure chance that the greatest of military captains have for the most part been young men.

Alexander conquered Persia before he was 25. Hannibal crossed the Alps before 29, and even Caesar when he completed the conquest of Gaul was only 44, this, after having subjugated Spain, several years before. As for Napoleon, whether we choose his victories at Lodi or the triumph before Austerlitz as his greatest achievement, he is still a man under, or but a little over 30, who has already reached the acme of his genius.

It thus appears that custom and social bias contrive, in many fields, to postpone the age at which an individual will be afforded recognition, and what is more serious, opportunity of doing the things he could do at the age at which he is most capable of doing them. These factors, to be sure, make themselves most felt in the case of statecraft (politics), religion, and the military arts in ordinary times. Their effect is less severe in the field of art, literature and science, where achievement is to a certain extent independent of social appraisal. On the other hand, in the case of literary and scientific productions, we must take into consideration the fact already mentioned, that the year in which an author's opus is completed does not necessarily represent the period of his most assiduous labors. When, therefore, to the foregoing fact we add that the throes of parturition have been preceded by a greater or shorter period of travail, it is apparent that the so-called dates of greatest achievement, if taken at their face value, are likely to give a false idea as to the age of greatest fertility. To do so would often lead to a type of error that might be made if we judged the merit of a great painting by the excellence of the artist's last stroke. Leonardo is said to have spent 14 years on *The Last Supper*, Dante no less than 20 on his *Divine Comedy*, and Darwin almost as long on his *Origin of Species*. Who can say at what moment they showed their greatest brilliance? The only thing that can certainly be asserted is that, with the completion of these works, these moments must already have passed. When due allowance is made for this discrepancy, it is my opinion that, using even such data as we have, a careful investigation would show that the acme of a man's intellectual and artistic virility, even when measured by the date of his magnum opus, would certainly be not much over 40, and probably much nearer to 35.

The conclusion which I have just drawn does not deny that there have been men of genius who have made great contributions in later life. History furnished many examples, and perhaps the most outstanding one of our days is that of Professor Freud who, at the age of 70, continues his remarkable labors. But even in his case, it must be admitted that his greatest single work, *The Interpretation of Dreams*, was completed when he was barely 40. The persistence of achievement in later life is perhaps in itself one of the sure signs of genius, but the contributions of a genius cannot be compared with that of the average man, for the output of genius in its dotage may still be superior to that of mediocrity in its prime. It is rather a comparison of earlier works of men of genius with their own later ones that must be undertaken. When this is done, the evidence is not in doubt. Even a layman can detect the wide gap between the Shaw that wrote *Candida* 1898) and the one who wrote *The Apple Cart* (1931).

It would be a laborious but not difficult task to show that the effect of age is to diminish the individual's creativeness in practically all realms of human endeavor. An examination of the rosters of the institutions which specialize in men who have "arrived," and their contributions after canonization, would, perhaps, be the shortest way to demonstrate this contention. The first that come to mind are the National Academies and Royal Societies of one type or another; but to these one must add many of the higher seats of learning, namely, the universities which, in thought as well as in politics, have historically been the bulwarks of conservatism. To the extent to which the old men in them have exercised influence upon scientific thought, they have been, in a large measure, responsible for the intolerance to new ideas which has usually characterized university learning. This, for example, is illustrated today by the attitude of the older psychologists to psychoanalysis which they reject just as the older physicists at first rejected the Copernican, and the older biologists, the Darwinian theories. Part of this opposition has an emotional basis, but part of it is due to a veritable inability to grasp a new idea. This disability is of course relative, but very real, and is to be understood to mean that they can no longer as easily see through a logical problem, in the same sense that a dull student cannot grasp a difficult Latin construction or an original problem in geometry.[1]

A satisfactory proof of this contention would of course require a systematic comparison of the abilities of the younger (men between 25 and 35) and older workers (50 and 60) in any given field, and I cannot say that I have made this investigation or that it would be possible to do so at present, with

[1] In the matter of sheer learning this superiority of youth has long, though grudgingly, been admitted. Professor Thorndike in his recent book on *Adult Learning*, has, it is true, seemed to refute this generalization, but his evidence, valuable as it be, is not very damaging; and this for two reasons. In the first place, his "old" students were not very old, being mostly under 35; in the second place, and this is the more important, his older students were a very selected group. They were individuals who came voluntarily to further what they thought as an insufficient education, and by this fact alone showed themselves to be above the general average. There is little proof that the results would have been the same had the studies been made on an unselected population.

any rigor. Fortunately, some ready made data is available to us in the roster of names of those who have made the greatest contributions to the new physics, which furnish almost conclusive confirmation of my contention. The new physics, and by this I mean the quantum and wave mechanics, is almost exclusively the work of young scientists: De Broglie,[1] Heisenberg,[2] Dirac,[3] Schroedinger,[4] Fermi,[5] to mention only the outstanding, are nearly all under 35, and some only in their twenties. It is true that they were inspired by the work of Planck, Bohr[6] and Einstein,[7] but the great discoveries of these geniuses were similarly made when they too were relatively young men.

The decline of vigor with age, which the above adduced facts show to be the general rule in the field of intellectual endeavor, is even more apparent in the realm of affective life, although it is less easy to marshall numerical evidence for the conclusion. But the absence of statistical proof is more than compensated by the accumulated experience of mankind, whether as revealed in the homely assertions of the practical man, the guarded reflections of the physician[8] or

[1] De Broglie, Prince Louis, derived the wave properties of matter in 1925, at the age of 33.

[2] Heisenberg, Werner, founder of the quantum matrix mechanics, promulgated when its author was in his twenties.

[3] Dirac, P. A. M., at 24 discovered the relativistic quantum equations and predicted the existence of the positive electron which was experimentally discovered 3 years later.

[4] Schroedinger, Edwin, founder of the wave mechanics (1926) when he was in his late thirties.

[5] Fermi, E., born in 1902, who with Dirac discovered a quantum statistics named after them.

I am indebted for this information to my friend, Mr. Alexander W. Stern, himself one of the important younger American mathematical physicists.

[6] Bohr, Neils. His work on the quantum theory appeared in 1915. He was then in his early thirties.

[7] Einstein's first paper on relativity appeared when he was only 26.

[8] See for example the famous remarks of Osler in his 1905 address at the Johns Hopkins University. The speech is quoted at length in "His Life," by Harvey Cushing. The following excerpts give the general tenor of his attitude

the penetrating observations of the great poets. However, for those who insist upon objective evidence, one may point to such facts of physiology, as that, with age, breathing becomes harder, the heart slower, and the general reactions of the body more sluggish, just as our senses become more blunted. Indeed the statement that we grow cold with age is literally true. The temperature of the body is nearly a whole degree less at 60 than at 10, and when we recall that a fall of two degrees usually occurs when the organism is not far from death, the possible significance of the decrease, small as it is, becomes somewhat alarming.

More facts might be cited, but apart from the fact that the multiplication of instances does not *per se* establish a proposition, the addition of more examples is hardly likely to augment the credence of the reader if he has not before this been convinced by evidence already presented. I say this, because in presenting my observations orally, I have often noted that, when an auditor was unimpressed by the first

---

toward the influence of age on our abilities: "I have two fixed ideas . . . . which have a direct bearing on this important problem. The first is the comparative uselessness of men above forty years of age. This may seem shocking, and yet read aright the world's history bears out the statement. Take the sum of human achievement in action, in science, in art, in literature—subtract the work of the men above forty, and while we should miss great treasures, even priceless treasures, we would practically be where we are today. It is difficult to name a great and far-reaching conquest of the mind which has not been given to the world by a man on whose back the sun was still shining. The effective, moving, vitalizing work of the world is done between the ages of twenty-five and forty—these fifteen golden years of plenty, the anabolic or constructive period, in which there is always a balance in the mental bank and the credit is still good. In the science and art of medicine, young or comparatively young men have made every advance of the first rank. Vesalius, Harvey, Hunter, Bichat, Laennec, Virchow, Lister, Koch—the green years were yet upon their heads when their epoch-making studies were made. To modify an old saying, a man is sane morally at thirty, rich mentally at forty, wise spiritually at fifty—or never. . . . .

"My second fixed idea is the uselessness of men above sixty years of age, and the incalculable benefit it would be in commercial, political, and in professional life if, as a matter of course, men stopped work at this age."

array of facts (as was usually the case), the addition of further evidence served rather to repel than win him over to the point of view advanced. Usually they merely elicited a counter citation of examples of superior performance in old age; but, even when the evidence was accepted, the conclusion was generally rejected. One person put it thus: "Your facts seem correct, but somehow I feel you must be wrong." Seeking to discover the basis for this negative reaction, I have myself gotten the feeling that it was largely due to what Professor Spearman has called "the alarming consequences" which the view that our abilities decline with old age, seems to imply. "The suggestion arises," he says, "that a man becomes too old for his work, not at 70 or even at 50 but already at 30." And some of the alarming consequences which he fears are that, "the boy or girl on quitting school, instead of as now proceeding to work his or her way up in the world would everywhere. . . straightway assume command," and "thenceforward, as gradually as may be, plane downwards." The answer to all this is that it is just a fancied specter of a frightened psychologist and not a necessary corollary to the unadorned conclusion. It may be true that human capacities attain their zenith before the age of 30, and yet it need not follow that boys and girls in their twenties be put at the helm of our social, industrial, and political ships, for the simple reason that successful operation of these enterprises does not depend upon native ability alone. There are, of course, other factors,—tested knowledge and experience, to mention only the most common, which may be more important, and these, of course, take time to acquire. One may, for example, concede far greater intelligence to a young physician just out of medical school, and yet legitimately have more confidence in a less gifted old practitioner, because of the latter's greater experience. In practical life particularly, the situations that arise are often too complicated, and the need for prompt action too urgent, to permit elaborate examination of the problem at hand. What is needed here is quick recognition of the difficulty, and an acquaintance with consequences of past results in similar situations; and this knowledge accrues with age. All this may be termed experience, and I have, of course, not argued that experience is a negligible factor in practical life, although my personal view is that its importance is greatly exaggerated.[1]

Again, the fact that man's capacities reach their zenith at 30 does not necessarily mean that he becomes "too old" for work at 50. It simply means that at 50 he is probably beyond the age at which he can do his best work, and may only imply that he ought to switch to a less creative, a less energy-demanding job. That is a more obvious conclusion and, if its cogency is overlooked, it is seemingly because its logic is obscured by some emotional factor, most often, the harrowing phantasy of the dismissed pilot or the discharged employee. This fear has in recent years been augmented by the callousness with which many industrial organizations have treated their older workmen, and the spectre has arisen as to what would happen if the practice of dismissing or penalizing with reduced wages, workers who, after years of service, have become less efficient (or if you wish, less economic), were extended. Now, my personal view is that faithful service ought not thus be rewarded; society should be beholden to its workers for what they have already done, and not measure its rewards by the value of their immediate services alone; we do as much for race-horses, why not for men? There is a happy medium between dismissing a pilot with Teutonic brutality,

[1] One might point out, en passant, that the general effect of relying on experience in practical life, is to eliminate thought and obviate inquiry. The "experienced" man knows what things "work" and what's "the right thing to do," because he "knows what's going to happen," or has seen such cases before. As the practical man usually only does what's been tried and proved, such knowledge is extremely valuable. It makes the world go round, as the saying is. But while experience may make the world go round, it cannot make it go forward. For this intelligence is necessary.

and retaining him in oriental fashion beyond his usefulness, because of sentimental ancestor worship. For example, social insurance might well see to it that no man after giving the best twenty to thirty years of his life to a job be requited with an insecure old age or an insulting part-pension. But all this is beside the point. We may resent the callousness of a social structure for denying security to old age, but the way to combat it is not by insisting that older men are just as efficient or or even just as useful. They are not.

We may profitably stop here, lest by laying disproportionate emphasis on certain speculative inferences, the direct conclusions of the facts themselves be lost in a maze of controversy which a discussion of their practical implications is likely to arouse. These facts, namely the age curves presented in the preceding pages, supplemented by certain data derived from biographical studies of men of genius show: (1) that the native capacities of most men tend to attain their maximum between the ages of 22 and 28 years, and in some cases even earlier; (2) beginning with about age 25, there starts a steady decline in both physical and intellectual vigor which increases progressively with advancing age; (3) the decline between 25 and 40 years is relatively small, but nevertheless perceptible, and does not justify the belief that there is even an approximate maintenance of vigor over any considerable number of years; (4) there is no evidence whatsoever for the belief that the average man maintains either his intellectual or physical vigor to the end of his natural life (50th year and beyond), even when spared from the ravages of disease; (5) the age-curves of such mental abilities as have been measured indicate that intellectual capacity, contrary to current belief, begins to decline earlier rather than later than most physical capacities.

If the foregoing generalizations are correct, it is apparent that many of our current views regarding the relation of age to ability are in need of drastic revision; also such social customs as may be directly based upon them. It is not true, as a popular writer has proclaimed, that "life begins at forty," except perhaps for those who have wasted a great part of it before. It is, however, a regrettable fact that much of our social organization today, both for historical and contemporary reasons, is conducive to just such waste; that our educational system is progressively adding years to the age at which an individual is permitted to strike out for himself without furnishing him the training it is supposed to give him, and our industrial system, by its increased mechanization, condemning large portions of the population to types of activity which offer but little opportunity for individual enterprise and creative expression. The whole problem of the meaning and value of experience in relation to achievement needs to be reinvestigated. In certain fields it is clearly overestimated (e.g., in the scientific professions), in others equally disregarded (politics). Present day conventions as to the ages when men are admitted to, and when retired from, certain positions are largely arbitrary. There is little scientific ground for making 30 years the minimal age for admission to the Senate and only 25 that to the House of Representatives, or the age of retirement from the army 60, from a university, 70, and that from the supreme court the personal opinion of the incumbent. The facts which we have collected in the preceding pages ought to enable us to decide more intelligently. Of course, ability alone is not the only factor which needs to be taken into consideration, but the least a knowledge of the relation of age to physical and intellectual virility can do will be to keep us from giving false reasons for right actions.

CHAPTER VIII

GENIUS AND DEFICIENCY

The title of this chapter may be a bit misleading. My intention is not to inquire whether genius is or is not, as some writers have held, a special pathological condition allied to one or another form of morbidity, but to extend the investigation already begun as to the manner in which the very superior and the very handicapped differ from those who are neither the one nor the other. In thus stating the problem, I may seem to have assumed what in fact ought to be first proved, namely that genius is a species of ability (and degeneration only an extreme lack of it), but as the elaboration of the implied definition will occupy our attention for the greater part of this chapter the reader will perhaps pardon a brief anticipation of a conclusion to which I believe the evidence on the subject inevitably commits us.

To state unequivocally in a sentence or even a paragraph just what types of ability or what traits an individual must possess in order to merit being called a genius is an extremely difficult, if not an impossible task. Nor is the task of defining degeneration categorically less onerous. Here as elsewhere it is easier to furnish undisputed examples than to give an all inclusive definition. Da Vinci, Shakespeare, Pasteur, Edison are individuals who under any definition would be included under the group genius, and a visit to any large institution for defectives would furnish equally obvious examples of degeneration. The difficulty only begins when one tries to state categorically how they differ from those who are neither; and after reviewing the efforts of those who have felt it necessary to do so, one is forced to conclude that very little is to be gained by the attempt. This is inevitable because genius is what the

German philosophers call a *Grenzphänomen*,—a limiting phenomenon; and in the definition of such ultimates we can only emulate the wisdom of St. Augustine when asked to define time, and answer with him, "I know it when you ask me not."

The task is not so difficult if instead of insisting on a categorical we are content with a working definition. Any good dictionary will then meet our needs, and it is such a one,[1] for example, that Galton made use of when attacking the problem in "*Hereditary Genius*." On the other hand, one does well to avoid the nimble phrases of the essayist, and the ostensibly profounder but only more heavy footed ones of the philosopher. There is a strong temptation to be intrigued by such laconicisms as that "genius is the infinite capacity to take pains" (Carlyle), or that it "is simply the completest objectivity"[2] (Shopenhauer). But any attempts to apply them very quickly reveals their inadequacy, for like copy-book maxims they are more true in their breach than in their exemplification.

By suggesting recourse to a good dictionary for a working definition, I do not of course intend to set up the lexicon as the final arbiter as to what genius is, but merely to imply that such a definition, to the extent that it is not bound up with any special theory, will generally enable us to include all or nearly all individuals which we may wish to so classify, whatever our ultimate conception of the nature of genius may be. From this point of view, as good a definition of genius as I have found is the one given by Baldwin,[3] which with slight modification may be stated as follows: "Genius is superiority of ability in an unusual degree;" and a person of genius is one

[1] Johnson's Dictionary. In this connection Galton wrote (Preface, second edition, London, 1892): "There was not the slightest intention on my part to use the word genius in any technical sense, but merely as expressing an ability that was inborn and superior."

[2] The rest of this gem of confusion reads: "that is, objectivity of the mind as opposed to subjectivity, in other words, the selfish will." *The World as Will and Idea*. Quoted by Turck (93).

[3] Dictionary of Philosophy and Psychology, vol. 1, p. 450.

"whose mental, moral or artistic capacity or achievement is of extraordinarily high quality or value."

Using the terms mental, moral and artistic in their widest sense, this definition does not commit us to any special theory of genius, but only imposes upon us the task of furnishing a satisfactory criterion for the delimitation of the groups we propose to call "superior" and "able in an unusual degree." The task is not an easy one, and in what follows I propose to examine some of the more important efforts made, restating what I believe to be the crux of the problem as well as what seems to me a satisfactory solution of it.

Another point, however must first be clarified; or, more precisely, a possible objection removed: It might be argued that our definition, in spite of its air of objectivity, nevertheless contains an unwarranted assumption. Thus one may urge that the assertion that genius is a kind of ability or capacity, albeit a superior one, is itself only a theory. A number of writers on the subject have in fact so insisted, most recently Hirsch (36), who with some show of contempt has referred to the definition of genius in terms of ability as the "talent" theory of genius. So far as I have been able to see, however, the arguments advanced by these writers against this definition amount in the end to little more than so much hair-splitting. For when we finally come to what these writers have to offer as their own particular differentiae of genius, they turn out to be only some especially esteemed trait or ability with a mystic label attached to it: "Complete objectivity," "directed intuition," "love of truth," etc. Hirsch calls it, "creative intelligence." The fact which gives such definitions a semblance of truth is that they are generally applied to eminence in fields of achievement where evaluation is largely subjective, and objective measurement often impossible. The most favorable and, accordingly, most commonly cited instances are those of great men in the fields of religion and politics. With regard to these, writers are wont to point out that when measured with the ordinary yardsticks of ability, e.g., excellence of memory, degree of physical endurance and courage, or even amount of general intelligence, men of genius may differ but little from the average individual, and that it is only when certain intangible traits or special aspects of personality are posited, that their genius may be explained. But even granting that some special potentialities or kinds of endowment are prerequisites for genius, it does not follow that these qualities, whatever they may be, are necessarily entirely absent in ordinary mortals. It may be true that the genius of Christ was his divine personality, but it nevertheless remains true that there are at least some men (not geniuses) who are Christlike; and if that of Lincoln was his supreme humanity, there are not a few in this world who may legitimately be called humane. The point is that those qualities, aspects of personality, and character, or whatever else may be ultimately posited as the *sine qua non* of genius, will be found in some degree, however small, in all men. There is no evidence at all for such claims as those advanced by Hirsch that genius "is another psychological species differing as much from man in his mental and tempermental processes as man differs from the ape."[1] Accounts by men of genius as to their mental process in doing creative work or arriving at great discoveries[2] reveal little that will not be found in the testimony of ordinary mortals of their own small efforts.

I believe that the mainspring of the *sui generis* theories of genius is their authors' failure to perceive that qualitative changes may result from purely quantitative variations or differences in rate of change in the same process or phenomenon. A savage who has never seen anything freeze, might well esteem ice and water as two entirely different substances, and, to the extent that they present different physical properties, his classification of them as such would be quite correct,

[1] Loc. cit., p. 298.

[2] See for example Poincaré's recital of his discovery of the Fuchsian functions. Science et Méthode (75), chapter III.

but that does not alter the fact that ice is only water at its freezing point. Similarly, even a sophisticated individual unless acquainted with the facts of chemistry would find it hard to believe that the rusting of a bar of iron and the burning of a piece of wood involve one and the same process. And so of a great many other facts of physics, the most dramatic of which are perhaps those which occur when substances change their state, or undergo sudden transformation, as in the case of volitalization, crystallization, etc. But, all these "changes" involve no new process. The nature of heat (increased molecular motion) which raises the temperature of water from 66 to 68 degrees is the same as that which raises it from 98 to 100 degrees Centigrade, only that the increased evaporation which was imperceptible at the former point becomes conspicuous at the latter. Steam is only water at its boiling point. The striking thing between water at 68 degrees and water at its boiling point is not the difference in its intrinsic nature, but in its practical value. Steam under right pressure will propel a 5,000 ton locomotive, and a thousand times a like *quantity* of water at 68 degrees will not propel a toy engine.

It is the same with human capacities. Beyond certain points, even slight differences in efficiency of an individual's ability may so alter the character of the resulting performance as to make it appear an achievement of an entirely different order or even kind. Thus, if we compared the manual dexterity of the skilled performer who does sleight of hand tricks, and the similar dexterity of the novice who has just not arrived at the point where he can make the coin disappear imperceptibly into his sleeve, actual measurements of their speed of movement would show very slight quantitative difference. In fact as little as 5/100ths of a second in speed of reaction time might be all that separates the two, but this slight superiority, coupled with our ignorance to explain it, makes of the one a tyro and of the other a magician.

The situation is no different when we come to intellectual

feats. Lightning calculators astound us, of course, but their feats only consist of doing superbly and quickly what most of us can do only tolerably well and at a much smaller speed. The arithmetical process involved in multiplying 5 by 5 place numbers is not essentially different from that involved in getting the products of 2 by 2 place numbers, though individual calculators have always hit upon short cut methods. But any one who has read the great Bidder's account of his own phenomenal skill will agree with him that his genius in this field was not due to any demoniacal gift, but could be explained readily on the basis of an intelligible difference of ability or improved method. It is the same with literary and artistic genius. To be sure, there are some other very real differences between the novels of a Henry Fielding and the feuilletons of a Grub Street hack, but these do not derive from any specificity of contents or material. It is, of course, true that great writing, as has often been pointed out, raises us to emotional heights and stirs us in ways which mediocre efforts ordinarily do not. But so may a very mediocre religious hymn or even an illiterate war song. We cannot therefore ascribe this effort exclusively to the writing itself, certainly not to any of its segregable elements. On the contrary, when we examine the stuff out of which similar types of literary material are made, there is found a direct kinship and continuity of ability. This continuity becomes more obvious, if instead of making comparison between extremes of ability, for example, between those displayed in a Hamlet with those of a nondescript morality play, we make the comparison between some of the lesser, yet still great Shakespearean plays and those of his Elizabethan contemporaries, (Marlowe, Kidd, Fletcher), able dramatists, but still not of the order that would place them in the genius class. These differences are then clearly seen to be those of degree and not of kind. *The Merchant of Venice* is definitely superior to the *Jew Of Malta*, but in no respect can they be said to be so distinct as to warrant our asserting that they belong to separate "species."

If the foregoing observations are correct, we are compelled to reject all explanations of genius which call for the intercession of a mystical something, a superhuman touch or *sui generis* traits, that is, all "divine-spark theories." On the other hand, we are compelled by the same facts to look for an explanation of genius in terms of some sort of superiority or unusualness in degree of ability, for the simple reason that we have no alternatives. There are, however, two ways in which superiority or unusualness of degree may be interpreted. According to the first and purely statistical definition, originally proposed by Galton, a genius is one who with respect to any ability or group of abilities, falls among the highest X- per cent of individuals, or attains a certain standing (mathematically defined) with respect to these traits and abilities when ranked according to some order of merit. According to the second which we may call the *theory of critical differences,* genius, while still a summary term for unusual superiority, also implies a qualitative distinction,—a distinction which arises not because we are dealing with a new species of ability, but from the fact that when human capacities surpass certain levels of performance, the achievements to which they give rise, may take on altered characteristics. The assumption here is that these alterations are analogous to the transformations that occur in material substances at certain critical points of (pressure, temperature, etc.) where small changes in cause may produce striking changes in effect. The second explanation, I believe, more nearly covers all the facts, and I shall presently state the arguments which favor it. But first, a few more words on the possible meanings which may be assigned to the concept of superiority (or unusualness), of ability, which enter into and form part of the theory.

The concept of superiority as it enters into the definition of genius has a three-fold connotation. There is first the general comparative connotation of *very-much-more-than,* to a superlative degree. The superior person is one who can do very much more of, or very much more quickly, or very much better, the kind of thing which the average person can do only in a moderate degree. This is the aspect which we referred to as ability to extraordinary degree. Secondly, the superior person is a rare person. He is one in a hundred, or one in a thousand, or one in a million, etc. This is the aspect of ability implied by the term "unusualness." Finally the superiority of an individual, to warrant the classification of genius, must be in a field or a type of performance which is humanly esteemed in and for itself. This is necessary to exclude such extraordinary and unusual performances as sitting forty days on top of a telegraph pole, and records in pie eating contests. Human endeavors and achievements seem to arrange themselves into a sort of ascending or descending hierarchy of aesthetic importance. Poetry, music, mathematics,—all the arts and sciences, etc., are fields in which men may merit the name of genius, but not at eating, drinking, or remembering telephone numbers. And even in the several arts and sciences themselves, there is, and to my mind justly so, a kind of order of worthwhileness; so that, to take music as an example, a man is more likely to merit the name of genius by composing a symphony than writing a *jazz* song. Of course, different ages may esteem differently the various endeavors of men, just as the progress of the arts and sciences may alter the objects toward which their energies are directed, but there is no doubt that, in spite of these differences, human achievement does lend itself to at least a rough hierarchical arrangement or classification with respect to its worthwhileness or significance.

So much for the chief differentiae of genius. These are, of course, not the only characteristics by which it may be distinguished. Men of genius have other outstanding traits, like great zeal, abundance of energy, and capacity for work; but it would be beyond our purpose to enter into any description of their personal characteristics. Nor can we enter here into a review of the special theories of genius, which have varied all the way from the naïve physiological conceptions of

Flechsig to the purely spiritual interpretations of Meyers.[1] So also, must we omit the interesting question as to the relative importance of nurture and nature in the production of genius. More pertinent to our discussion is how men of genius, however produced, may be detected. What sort of achievement must an individual attain to be rated a genius?

The first one who attempted to solve this problem in a scientific manner was Francis Galton. His answer was simplicity itself: Men of genius are those who become illustrious, or who attain great eminence in their work, as judged by the reputations they achieve. He then proceeded to define in both a statistical and social way what he meant by eminent, illustrious and reputation. "An eminent man was one who achieved a position attained by one person in four thousand, an illustrious man one who achieved a position attained by only one in each million." The genius belonged to the latter class. They were men "whom the whole intelligent part of the nation mourns when they die; who, deserve a public funeral; and who rank in future ages as historical characters." Reputation, he defined, as "the opinion of contemporaries revised by posterity, the result of critical analysis of each man's character by many biographers." All of which criteria, it will be seen, conform to the differentiae of genius which we have laid down, namely superiority of ability, rarity of incidence, and pursuit of a type of activity that is socially esteemed and considered worthwhile by those who are qualified to judge.

Of the three criteria, the last has been the most difficult to apply objectively. The difficulty is again a practical one, and resides in the squeamish problem of arriving at an undisputable and unequivocal basis for one's ultimate choices of those to be included among the truly illustrious. Galton in his

[1] A very excellent summary of the more important theories will be found in *Theories of Genius* by Woodbridge Riley (79). On the relation of genius to insanity, see Nesbit, F. F. *Insanity of Genius* (67).

study of *Hereditary Genius,* made up his list from the names in the then standard biographical dictionary, assuming that the very fact that a person had been included was in itself proof of his having attained some legitimate degree of eminence; and those who have since applied his method (Cattell, Thorndike, Cox et. al.) have followed similar procedures. Cattell thought to make the method more objective not only by using several encyclopedias instead of a single source, but by further ranking his selections in terms of the amount of space given them in the various sources. This, to be sure, makes for greater objectivity, but it is to be noted that the improvement is due to the averaging of the opinions of a greater number of authorities rather than to the taking into account the amount of biographical space devoted to the individuals. Indeed, the space criterion alone would often lead to egregious errors, since the amount of space devoted to various persons (particularly historical characters) not only depends upon their own merit, but also their historical associations and human interest appeal. Thus in Cattell's *First Study on the Statistics of Eminent Men,* the relatively mediocre Napoleon III when judged by the amount of space devoted to his biography ranks along side of Shakespeare, Luther, and Plato, among the ten most illustrious persons of all time, whereas the great Gauss is some eight thousand names behind him. So also, the inconsequential George Sand is put in the same company with such giants as Cervantes and Rabelais, whereas Beethoven, Mamonides and Aesop, are far down the list. By the same method, Nero is more illustrious than Marcus Aurelius and Swedenborg a greater man than Copernicus. These distortions show the dangers of trusting too much to historical estimates as well as the fallacy of identifying fame with ability. But it would be erroneous to assume, on that account, that the entire method is faulty. What it does seem to indicate is that a true order-of-merit ranking of men of genius cannot be had from an analysis of biographical dictionaries, however refined. The statistical method is valid, but cannot go beyond the reliability of the data to which it is applied, that is, the competency of those whose estimates are being collated. Here one man's opinion is not as good as another's, and what is needed is a preliminary selection of authorities whose estimates and modes of expressing them will be relatively free from the handicaps[1] inherent in or imposed upon authors of encyclopedic articles. Probably the most satisfactory procedure of arriving at a true order of merit of men of genius would be to entrust their selection and ranking to experts in their respective fields, that is, the men and women who at the time are themselves doing eminent work in the same fields.[2]

The topic of deficiency and degeneration from a range-of-human-capacities point of view presents the same problems as those which we have been discussing in the case of genius. This follows from our conception that degeneration or deficiency like genius is a matter of quantitative differences. But here again, as in the case of genius at the upper extreme, while adhering to the view that defectives are those who with respect to any trait or ability fall at the lowest extreme of achievement as regards that capacity, I do not maintain that that is the only characteristic of deficiency. Deficiency is also "qualitative" in character. But this qualitative aspect arises not from the fact that defectives are a class *sui generis*, but from the fact that human abilities when they fall below certain levels of achievement acquire new characteristics or if you will, *Gestalten*. A mental defective is not only a person who has less of the same thing (e.g., intellectual ability) than a person of "dull normal" intelligence, but one who shows a type of behavior which also appears to be qualitatively different. The same may be said with regard to differences

[1] E.g., nationalistic bias.

[2] Professor Cattell has attempted just such a procedure in ranking the thousand most eminent persons in his *American Men of Science* (12).

between a moron and an imbecile, etc., as any person with clinical experience can testify. They actually "look" and "act" differently. And these differences in "looks" and "behavior" can be explained by assuming that human intelligence when passing certain points takes on new configurations which for phenomenological reasons we find it convenient to recognize as different totalities.

The topics of genius and degeneration are only special cases of the more general problem involved in the evaluation of human capacities, namely the question of quantitative versus qualitative differences. There are those who insist that all such differences are qualitative, and those who with equal conviction maintain that they are exclusively quantitative. The true answer is that they are both. General intelligence, for example, is undoubtedly quantitative in the sense that it consists of varying amounts of the same basic stuff (e.g., mental energy) which can be expressed by continuous numerical measures like Intelligence Quotients or Mental-Age scores, and these are as real as any physical measurements are. But it is equally certain that our description of the difference between a genius and an average person by a statement to the effect that he has an I.Q. greater by this or that amount, does not describe the difference between them as completely or in the same way as when we say that a mile is much longer than an inch. The genius (as regards intellectual ability) not only has an I.Q. of say 50 points more than the average person, but in virtue of this difference acquires seemingly new aspects (potentialities) or characteristics. These seemingly new aspects or characteristics, in their totality, are what go to make up the "qualitative" difference between them. It is the same with the totality of characteristics of intellectual capacity which we distinguish by such terms as "normal, moron, imbecile, etc., and probably also of many intermediate degrees or configurations of intelligence which for practical purposes we may not find useful to single out.

The interpretation I have advanced for these qualitative differences is that they are the result of transformations consequent to the passing of certain critical points of achievement assumed to exist in all human capacities. Genius and degeneration are but two such critical points, of special interest because of their practical and social importance, but only illustrating a general phenomenon or principle, namely, the principle that quantitative variations may give rise to qualitative differences. These critical points, the occurrence of which in physical processes furnished us the basis of our analogy, cannot, to be sure, be definitely localized in the case of human capacities. It is furthermore possible, and indeed probable, that they are not fixed points, certainly not in the same sense as are the boiling and melting points of water, but the critical difference analogy does adequately sum up what is observed, or seems to occur. What the actual mechanisms of the transformations may be is at present hard to conjecture, but in purely psychological terms, one might say that, as a result of the change, a new configuration is produced. In this sense, the hypothesis of critical differences might be termed a configurational theory of human abilities.[1]

[1] The psychological principles of configurationism have as yet been but imperfectly described. It is only in the field of perception, as for example, in the laws of the "Gute Gestalt" of Wertheimer (105), that any definite progress has been made. Furthermore, the ultimate problem, as it concerns us here, is the nature of the dependency of the configurational whole upon its constituent parts. Here two general solutions are possible: One may say, as some have, that the *Gestalt* is itself the ultimate unit, that is, needs no further analysis into constituent elements, because it is for and of itself an indivisible whole. Or one may conceive every configuration as some function of the constituent elements. I am inclined to the latter view, and see no contradiction of thinking of a psychological configuration both as a unitary whole and variable function. Following the more recently advanced conceptions in atomic physics, one could say that psychological entities are configurations whose structures as wholes are at once dependent upon the absolute amount (or quanta) of energy, and the mode in which the quantities are arranged. The facts and assumptions needed would be similar to those involved in explaining the chemical properties of the different elements on the basis of

energy considerations (i.e., the number of electric charges which enters into the composition of their atomic structure).

According to these theories the chemical properties of the elements are given by their atomic numbers, that is, by the net positive charge of their nuclei. Helium differs from hydrogen by having one more net positive charge and hence one more bound negative electron revolving around its nucleus to balance it, lithium two more, beryllium three more, and so on down the list to the heaviest element, uranium, which has 91 bound negative electrons and accordingly an atomic number of 92. The interesting thing for us is that all these electrons as well as the protons in the nucleus are made up of the same fundamental stuff, namely charges of negative and positive electricity. It thus appears that the multifarious chemical properties of the different elements are a function or, as we might say, the result of the number of like particles of energy that enter into their composition. The only other thing that matters is their arrangement or configuration (Languimir). In brief, in the physical world all qualitative differences are ultimately reducible to quantitative changes. A new property or group of properties (for our purpose, a new quality) comes into being when a certain amount or quantum of energy is added to or subtracted from an already organized whole. This gives rise to a new organization which differs from the preceding only by the fact that it has more or less of the same kind of stuff differently arranged. I believe the same sort of thing happens in the case of mental energy, and by extension, in the case of the transformation termed qualitative, observed in the more complex systems we call human capacities. But, of course, all this is purely speculative.

CHAPTER IX

THE MEANING OF DIFFERENCES

As a child I was once greatly amused by two comedians who seemed able to evoke much mirth in their audience by the simple art of asking each other absurd questions, and then answering them with equally absurd irrelevancies. Finally one asked, what at the time appeared to me the most absurd of all: "How high is up?" His partner answered appropriately enough "a lot," and the audience again rolled with laughter. But I have since learned that many questions asked off the stage by scientists as well as laymen, though on superficial examination intelligible enough, turn out, on more careful appraisal, to be no less absurd, and the answers to them little more illuminating. Meaningless inquiry of this kind is especially rampant in discussions of human capacities, and it will enable us to understand better the reason why, if, before turning to the subject proper of this chapter, we pause a moment to consider a bit further the nature of the scientific problem which our thespian quip so pointedly sums up.

What is foolish about asking, "How high is up?" Obviously, the fact that, as used in the sentence, the word "up" has no definite meaning. But in this respect it differs only relatively from a great many ostensibly learned questions which historians, anthropologists and psychologists daily propound: "Was Napoleon a great man?" "Are Italians more excitable than Englishmen?" "Are the Teutonic races superior to the Latins?" Pages and even books have been written upon these and similar questions, but it is clear that any intelligible reply to them depends upon our ability to attach precise meanings to the words great, excitable, and superior,—a task no easier than defining up and a lot.

The problem boils down to this: In what way must we define our terms to give unequivocal meaning to our judgments, and more particularly, in order to make valid comparisons. The answer, in so far as it concerns comparisons between human capacities, is that they must be capable of numerical definition. If I am not in a position to measure persons whose statures I wish to compare, then, my statement to the effect that A is taller than B is on a par with the critic's statement that Shakespeare was a greater poet than Dante, or that Paris is more beautiful than New York. The reason the assertions do not appear to be so, apart from the fact that experience has shown that we are likely to be more biased in making statements about poets than body stature, is that yard sticks are available to test the latter and no measuring rod to check up on the former. But we must not confuse practical difficulties with theoretical limitations.

Numerical comparisons are of course not the only ones that can be made between persons or objects. If I present two lines to a subject, I may either give him a ruler with which to detect any difference between them, or merely ask him to compare them subjectively; but in the latter case he can only make a qualitative judgment. Now, qualitative judgments differ from quantitative ones (i.e., those that can be expressed by numbers) in several important ways. In the first place they are, as already mentioned, influenced to a far greater degree by irrelevant or disturbing factors. Thus, in the example just cited, the presence of other lines adjacent or near the lines being compared may entirely alter our judgment as to their relative lengths. If, for instance, to the ends of one of two equal lines I affix arrow heads pointing inwards, and to the ends of the other arrow heads pointing outwards, the former will be "shortened" and the latter "lengthened," that is, they will appear to be so. Psychologists explain these "false" judgments as optical illusions, and prove them to be so by using a ruler. But there are other kinds of illusions besides optical ones, and for many of these, unfortunately, we have as yet no rulers, that is, scientific means of detection.

Consider for example, such assertions as that Frenchmen are more civilized than Americans, or that Englishmen are "squarer" fighters than Italians. What proof have we that these are not illusions, occasioned among other reasons, in the case of the former, by such things as a special admiration for a particular kind of cuisine or architecture; in the latter, by a concept of sportsmanship which considers it cowardly to kick a man on the floor, but perfectly correct to maim him with a blow for life, providing you do it while he's standing up. It is clear that we can have none until we can measure the things we wish to compare, whether they pertain to such vague concepts as sportsmanship, or to those of a host of other traits and abilities which we call human capacities.

Qualitative judgments differ in yet another way from quantitative ones. They are indeterminate. If, to go back to our illustration, I present two lines to a subject and merely ask him to state which is the longer, his judgment may be correct, but I have no way of telling whether they differ from each other by an inch or a mile. The same uncertainty characterizes all judgments in which comparisons are expressed by such terms as bigger, higher, brighter, etc., and it makes no difference whether the things compared are physical objects or aesthetic feelings. Furthermore, so long as such judgments preponderate in any body of knowledge, it cannot be said to have attained the status of an exact science. For as Lord Kelvin so aptly put it, it is only, "When you can measure what you are speaking about and express it in numbers, (that) you know something about it, but when you cannot express it in numbers, your knowledge is of a meager and unsatisfactory kind."

This dictum of Lord Kelvin has been the inspiration of modern scientific research, as shown not only by the fact that all the physical sciences have become more and more mathematical, but by the invasion of fields of knowledge by mathematics, where it was formerly thought unnecessary, as for instance, of physiology and psychology. Numerical analysis in these fields has not been easy, but it can be achieved wherever it is possible, in one way or another, to transmute qualitative into quantitative judgments. This can sometimes be done by the use of statistical methods. A good example is furnished by the Weber-Fechner law in psycho-physics, which sums up the mathematical relation between the intensity of a stimulus and its psychological correlate, that is, the sensation it evokes. It states that the psychological intensity of a sensation is a logarithmic function of the intensity of the physical stimulus which induces it, and to the extent which the law holds we can express purely subjective judgments in quantitative terms. Thus in comparing two lights we can say one is twice or three times as bright as another, and by the use of a proper formula correct our judgments to a tolerable degree of accuracy. It then becomes possible to assert that an individual who is able to perceive a light of a certain intensity has an acuity of vision of twice or three times as great as that of another whose vision is less by a certain measurable amount. But in the case of a preponderant number of human traits and abilities we are far from able to do this. We have no way of calculating how much kinder B is than A, how much more civilized Europeans are than Burmans, how much more honest we may be than our neighbors.

That we cannot make judgments of the kind just enumerated with any certainty or even rational basis, has not prevented men from doing so. Indeed it is with respect to the significance of differences in such traits and abilities that men have expressed the most positive opinions. Modesty and tolerance seem to characterize those opinions of mankind where least necessary. Disagree with a man as to the relative food value of spinach and carrots, and the worst he will do is laugh at your ignorance (although the argument may readily be settled by consulting a text-book of physiology); but doubt for a moment that his wife is as exemplary as yours, and you make him an enemy for life. There must, therefore, be something else than mere differences of fact, of degree or amount, which determines our attitude toward human differences. That something is obviously our emotional attitude toward them, or more generally, our estimate of what they mean to us, whether as members of a political party, citizens of a country, adherents of a faith; as fathers, mothers, related ones; as artists, bankers or carpenters; and finally, perhaps most important of all, as human beings.

This brings us to the central theme of our discussion, and the reader may perhaps see more clearly now, why I began this chapter on the meaning of differences, by repeating the seemingly absurd question of "How high is up?" So long as our estimate of human differences is contingent upon an emotional attitude or more broadly an anthropomorphic point of view, all comparisons whether expressed in qualitative or quantitative terms, are just as indeterminate. If Frenchmen are short, as esteemed by Englishmen, and tall when described by Laplanders, then the words tall and short have no definite meaning even when these judgments are accompanied by figures as to the relative heights of the three nationalities considered. The question still remains what height must a man be to be considered tall, and how much less must he measure to be considered short.

This question is not a quibble, nor an attempt to repeat what is generally admitted though oftener disregarded, namely, that all judgments are relative. I do not mean merely to call attention to the fact that a dragon-fly is small when compared with an elephant and big when compared with a gnat; or even that the 93,000,000 miles that separate us from the sun are insignificant when we compare them to other interstellar distances; but to bring out, as clearly as I can, the difference between a fact and our evaluation of it, or as it concerns us here, the distinction between subjective and objective meanings of differences.

Failure to observe this distinction is largely responsible for the confusion that permeates much of the discussion regarding the meaning of human differences. The only way out, so far as I can see, is to define all differences numerically, and then agree by convention which numbers we shall consider "small" and which "large." This definition should not be arbitrary, but based on a scientific analysis of such data as were at hand, and could, of course, be altered at such times as the accumulation of new facts made any change in it necessary.

To this point of view one might oppose the objection that any convention would be unsatisfactory, because in the long run all differences must be interpreted relative to their particular significance or importance. I say might, because by raising it, the objector would indicate a failure to understand the gist of the argument that has been presented, which is precisely, that it is this particularity of the terms big, small, etc., that makes them useless as scientific concepts. The objection only substitutes new terms for those we have already rejected, as may be readily seen by asking in turn: "significant" to whom? "important" for what purpose? Any particular answer would involve an anthropomorphic stand, and throw us back for a reconsideration of our original problem.

Forcing a man to hold his breath for three minutes may mean his death, whereas making him hold up his arm for an equally long period only a little fatigue; but these consequences are entirely irrelevant when our main concern is the comparative duration over which we can perform either. If a biologist studying the effect of atmospheric pressure on a particular species of protozoa found that three atmospheres merely retarded its movement and six snuffed out its life, we should hardly permit him to conclude that six atmospheres constituted an infinity, though the animalicule, if it could express itself, might.

The trouble, of course, is that when we come to interpreting human differences we are prone to identify ourselves more with the animalicule than with the biologist. We tend to estimate differences, not by their magnitude but by their effects. However justifiable such a point of view may be in practical situations, it becomes an inevitable source of confusion when introduced into scientific constructions. We must carefully distinguish, for instance, between the actual size of Cleopatra's nose and the consequences its length may have had upon the political destinies of the West. We may fully accept the contention that if it had been longer by as much as the thickness of a finger, the entire map of Europe would have been changed, without losing all ideas as to importance of metric dimensions. I am of course, not oblivious to the tragic, if not inordinate difference which a few millimeters added to a lady's nose may make in the scheme of things, but all that the Cleopatra fable can prove is that under certain circumstances, otherwise negligible, small differences may play a great rôle in the destiny of a human being or even a nation.

I do not wish to belabor the point under discussion. The object of the last, as well as of some of the earlier illustrations, has been to show that the problem of the meaning of human differences really presents two separate questions: one concerned with the magnitudes of these differences as such, the other with the subjective evaluation of these differences from some special, usually anthropomorphic point of view. This book has concerned itself primarily with the first of these two problems. It has done so because, in my opinion, the quantitative problem is the only one to which an unequivocal answer might be expected, and, in any case, because all attempts at evaluating human differences are necessarily dependent upon it. I shall, therefore, first restate what this answer is, and then conclude with what appear to me to be a few of the more useful correlaries that may be drawn from it.

The answer to the question as to the normal limits or range

of human capacities was given in chapter VI. It was there shown that the differences which separate the mass of mankind from one another, with respect to any one or all their abilities, are small—small in the sense that the ratios of the extremes of any given trait or ability, whenever measureable, could be expressed by small numbers. These numbers, the vast majority of which fall within the limits of 1.3 and 2.5, are not only small in the obvious sense that they fall at the very beginning of the infinite series of cardinal numbers, but in that, as compared with other ratios or orders of differences met with in nature, they are pitifully insignificant. In a world where forces, velocities and distances exist, which are thousands, nay millions of times as great as those of any others with which they may be compared, one cannot, except by sheer arbitrariness, fail to accede that the differences met with in human beings are any thing but insignificant. One need not turn to astronomy for contrasting examples; the realm of living things itself teems with illustrations. How small are the variations in human stature compared with those to be found in heights of trees, the differences in the physical strength amongst men when compared with that of the elephant, or of his speed of locomotion when matched with the flight of birds; or, to take a capacity in which man's own superiority is outstanding, of his intelligence when compared to the intellectual and learning abilities of even the higher animals. How picayune, indeed, do the figures and subsequent contentions of the anthropologist and psychologist appear when they insist upon the great significance of 4 per cent differences in cephalic index or 10 per cent difference in I.Q., when our research is not limited to an insignificant part of an insignificant portion of the universe entire of living things.

The reader may at this stage be willing to concede that the numerical differences observed in human capacities are small, but see little point in the fact because of his persistent conviction that it is not the magnitude of a difference but its effect that is important. The difference between 5 feet 11 inches and 6 feet 0 inches is admittedly small, but the ability to jump this extra inch may save a man's life; a lighted match may not possess much heat, but if thrown into a tank of gasolene may start a serious conflagration; and so forth. All of which is merely a reassertion of the not-to-be gainsaid generalization that "small causes may produce great effects." But this assertion is not as unequivocal as its simplicity would seem to indicate, and the failure to recognize its inapplicability to the argument at hand rests upon the ambiguous use of the terms cause and effect. A distinction must be made between what may be termed the physical and metaphysical, or as I prefer to call it, metaphorical usage of the terms. When it is asserted that a conflagration was "caused" by a lighted match, or an explosion of a gun by the blow of a small trigger hammer, the word cause merely means "necessary antecedent act." The match is not part of the conflagration, nor the blow of the trigger part of the explosion, much less of the destruction that may have ensued from either. A larger match would not have "caused" a bigger fire, nor a heavier blow a greater explosion. But, in other instances, the "cause" is part of the effect, in the sense that it cannot be separated from it. Such is the case in all physical processes that are connected by some "law," as when we say heat causes a body to expand, etc. Here the magnitude of the effect is directly related, that is, in some way proportional, to the magnitude of the cause, and shows no discontinuities, except that at certain "critical" points there may occur spectacular changes, as when at particular temperatures and pressures matter changes its state. These dramatic transformations, often following imperceptible variations, as when the addition of but a grain of a salt will cause an already saturated solution of it to crystallize, are also spoken of as great effects produced by small causes. Even here the word great is used in a metaphorical sense; the only true cases of the generalization, must be reserved for those instances where the relationship is such that a small variation in one of the variables produces a large variation in the others that are dependent upon it. Thus tripling the radius of a sphere increases its volume twenty seven fold, and an error of a fraction of an inch on the angular scale of a long range gun, may cause the marksman to miss his target by many miles.

Of the three ways just enumerated in which small causes may be said to produce great effects, it is only the first two that may be said to apply to human differences. Small variations in the realm of human capacities assume importance not because they are occasioned by any great quantitative changes, but because of certain esteemed qualitative differences to which they may give rise. Often these qualitative differences are not measurable at all, but assume importance only because of our subjective evaluation of them, that is, out of moral, esthetic or purely practical considerations.

In the realm of human affairs, differences however small intrinsically may be used as a basis of most divergent classifications and distinctions. Two per cent on an examination may be all, for example, that separates the man who passes from the man who fails a test, the result of which may start the one on a high career and condemn the other to a clerical job for life. Practical necessity may of course require that we establish arbitrary marks, lines or points, positions above or below which will be fraught with vital consequences; but it gives us no right to assume that the distances which separate individuals above and below these lines are necessarily great. No one indeed with any experience in the field of mental measurements would claim that there was any great difference in either the ability, knowledge, or anything else that a test purported to measure, between two candidates who scored 76 per cent and 74 per cent respectively on it. But, unfortunately, in every day life it is not by any measurable scores that the abilities and merits of individuals are compared, but by their social position, economic status, etc., however independent of actual ability, these may happen to be. It is no longer John Smith with a rating of 76 per cent against Tom Brown with only 74 per cent, but the Hon. Mr. Smith, Chief of Bureau, earning $20,000 a year, and just plain Tom Brown, clerk, $37.50 a week. The false implication is that Smith must have at least ten times as much ability as Brown.

In spite of the knowledge which precise mental measurements have thrown upon the range of human abilities, evaluation of differences between them is still largely on the basis of social position or economic status. It is true that kings are no longer regarded as miniature divinities, God's lineal descendants, nor priests as His special representatives on earth, but presidents of a republic, prime ministers, and international bankers, (when not in disrepute) become supermen with special endowments which place them apart from the common garden variety of men. So also, generals during war, movie stars, heavyweight champions, Supreme Court judges and United States Senators, and even college professors and columnists, though these in a lesser degree. Scientific investigation of the question, however, in no way substantiates this assumption, and offers little more to support the hero worship phantasies of a Carlyle or Nietsche than the deliberate trumperies of the modern publicity agent. On the contrary, the evidence is clearly against it. I do not merely base this conclusion on the obvious fact, that if we disregard the particular field in which the so called great show their virtuosity they become, for the most part, just ordinary mortals. I insist, more specifically, that within the very fields in which their superiority is conceded, the differences which separate them from the average man are small. To be sure, the schoolboy struggling with his elements of algebra seems eons away from the college professor who can solve differential equations, but that is only so long as the step between being able to solve a quadratic and differential equation is considered greater than that of being able to master algebra and of grasping the concept[1] of number at all. And that would be a very hazardous concession to make. For, while it is true that without the calculus we should never have discovered the wireless, nor arrived at a theory of relativity, we should be very much worse off if we didn't even know how to count. It is precisely this modest ability which all but separates man (as a reasoning creature) from the rest of the animal kingdom. The facts which we have gathered to show the range of human capacities, do not, of course, prove this; but they should do much to make us suspicious of those who, in order to glorify some of the selected members of our species, find it necessary to misinterpret the facts altogether.

[1] The concept of number here referred to is, of course, not the highly refined concept of the mathematical philosopher, but the simple idea of disparateness and the perception of the laws of commutation. A child may fully appreciate that $2 + 2 = 4$, in the sense that $4 = 1 + 1 + 1 + 1$, though it may require a Poincaré to prove it. Nor is this view inconsistent with the fact that, as now taught, the elementary concepts of number are for many children merely verbal habits; but psychological analysis will, I believe, reveal that these verbal habits ultimately acquire real meaning, in the sense that the child who has learned to count with match sticks will also be able to count pennies, and later make change correctly.

APPENDIX A

THE MEASUREMENT OF MENTAL ABILITY

In chapter II we considered the general conditions which had to be met for the quantitative measurement of human capacities and concluded that, in the case of most mental abilities, these conditions had not yet been fulfilled. More particularly the writer expressed the opinion that some of the recent statistical procedures offered as solutions of the problem were in fact no solutions at all. In view of the fact that this opinion is at variance with the views of some of the more distinguished workers in the field of mental measurements, it may be of some interest to pursue the subject at greater length, and the following pages are accordingly devoted to a more detailed discussion of the questions at issue.

The main difficulty in the measurement of mental abilities is the absence of any truly quantitative scales, that is, scales in which the successive units may be accepted as unequivocally equivalent. To say as much, however, is merely to restate the difficulty, not to explain it. We need to reach further back into the problem, in fact, begin with an analysis of the fundamental quantities in terms of which mental capacities as such are measured.

What, in fact, are these ultimate quantities? In general they are the things we call mental productions, i.e., the achievements or results of the mind's functioning. They are such things as perceiving objects, learning and retaining facts, solving arithmetical problems, comprehending spoken and written language, writing poetry, playing chess, designing machines, etc., to mention but a few of an almost endless list which might be made of human activities other than those involved in purely physiological functioning or bodily movement. For purposes of practical classifications these manifestations of mental functioning are generally grouped into a few broad, but not always mutually exclusive, classes; and, depending upon whether the general function or the productions are emphasized, we have such categories as reasoning, memory, imagination, intellectual ability, artistic ability, mechanical ability, etc. All this is largely a matter of convenience. The important thing is that in the end all mental capacities are known only through some concrete performance or production, and it is these productions which constitute the material or quanta (quantities) with which we have to deal. Thus, the quanta of mathematical ability are the various mathematical tasks performed or problems solved; of memory, the number of facts (sentences, digits, etc.), reproduced and recalled; of poetic ability, the poems actually written; and similarly, of all other capacities.

How now can these quanta be measured? If we follow the procedure employed in physics we should have to select in every case some definite production, and then express degrees of ability as multiples of this basic unit; thus, a person of good mathematical ability might be one that could perform a large number of arithmetical operations, solve many types of equations in algebra or theorems in geometry; a person of poor memory, one who retains relatively few facts, etc.; a great poet one who had written very many or very long poems, etc. It is clear, however, that amount or extent of production is not a sufficient criterion for the judgment of ability. If it were, Longfellow would have to be judged a greater poet than Coleridge, and many a routine calculator a greater mathematician than Newton. In evaluating ability, the excellence or difficulty of a production obviously also enters into our final estimates of it. In short, it makes quite a difference whether the arithmetical problem solved is of the order "If two apples cost five cents what will ten apples cost?", or that of deriving the law of inverse squares; whether the lyrics produced are the doggerels of a "jazz" song, or the type immortalized by a Heine or Shelley. Finally, there is the matter of time required to produce a given achievement. Of two individuals who perform the same task with equal merit, the one who does it in a shorter time is, in virtue of this fact alone, judged to be the more able.

The evaluation of mental capacities thus involves the measurement of three separate factors: (1) the excellence or difficulty of a production, (2) its magnitude or amount, and (3) the time required to perform it. Of these the last named, i.e., speed, can generally be measured directly, it being nearly always possible to record the exact time required to perform a given task, at least under test conditions. The second, i.e., the magnitude or amount of a production will lend itself to direct measurement only occasionally, i.e., when it can be broken up into commensurable parts of equivalent difficulty or merit. But merit and difficulty themselves cannot be measured directly. Thus, assuming that arithmetical ability is measured perfectly by skill at addition, then the number of seconds it takes two individuals to add a given number of examples of equal difficulty would be a direct measure of their respective arithmetical capacities. Conversely, the time being constant, the number of examples correctly added within a set period would be a similar measure, provided, of course, as already mentioned, the successive examples did not differ from each other as to difficulty. This latter assumption for instance, might be made with a fair degree of confidence, if the examples used were simple additions of two one-place numbers; even more secure would the assumption be, if the ability could be measured by such a simple task as that of canceling the number three on a uniformly printed sheet of digits arranged in chance order. On the other hand, the assumption would be very doubtful if, instead of simple additions, one used examples involving all the four arithmetical processes; and entirely invalid, if the test items were general problems in arithmetical reasoning. For, in the last named case, it is pretty certain that, unless some special method had previously been employed to equate them, no two successive problems, barring accidental coincidence, could be expected to be of identical difficulty.

The question of the measurement of difficulty, and the methods of transmuting qualitative to quantitative units which it represents, thus turns out to be the central problem of the measurement of mental capacities as a whole. A detailed consideration of it, however, would take us too far afield, and in view of Professor Thorndike's exhaustive treatment of the subject,[1] would be unnecessarily repetitious; but it will be useful to summarize the main efforts that have been made towards its solution.

Divested of their unessential particularities, the various attempts at transmuting qualitative estimates of difficulties and excellence of performance may be reduced to three methods or procedures. There is, first, the method which may be termed the *method of expert opinion.* Two tasks or mental performances are accepted as equally difficult or excellent, or one as harder, better, etc., than another to such and such a degree, when so judged by those who are supposed to know. Thus, one way of determining the probable difficulties of various mental tasks would be to have a competent psychologist[2] rate them; of an arithmetical problem, by submitting it to an experienced teacher of mathematics; of the excellence of a poem, by calling upon a poet of established reputation; of the merit of a picture, by relying onthe judgment of an art critic, and so on. This method, arbitrary and subjective as it may appear at first, is at once both a starting point and a final criterion of difficulty or excellence. It cannot be replaced by statistical methods, but only refined by them.

Statistical methods, however, do enable one to convert

[1] The Measurement of Intelligence (89).

[2] In actual practice, not one, but several.

purely subjective ratings into forms of data which will lend themselves to arithmetical treatment. Thus, by averaging the ratings of a reasonable number of competent judges we can arrive not only at the fact that two problems are equally difficult, (or two compositions are of equal excellence), but, after we have submitted a sufficiently large number of problems, be able to rank them in some ascending or descending order of merit. Such ordered ranking of any considerable number of performances will give a series of measures of relative position, i.e., a series in which the ordinal position of any item enables one to state whether it is more or less difficult than any item below or above it. It does not, however, enable us to say by how much. To do the last, one should further have to be able to convert such a series of relative position into a scale with equal units of amount. The question is, whether this may or may not be done. The consensus of opinion among psychologists today is that it is possible, and one may now find in various books on mental statistics formulae and tables whereby this can ostensibly be accomplished. My personal view is that the authors are mistaken; that while the statistical measures indicated do enable one to transmute measures of relative positions into measures of amount to the extent that they will now lend themselves to arithmetical treatment, the new scales thereby obtained do not consist of truly *equal* units of amount, in the same sense that successive units in the physical scale are equal. The fallacy of the various methods employed consists in assuming that units of variability are real in the same sense as inches, pounds and seconds are real. Whereas, in point of fact they are only mathematical differences of certain arithmetical relationships that obtain between the individual measures of a collection when grouped and treated in certain ways.[1]

[1] Experience has shown that the frequency with which measures of mental and physical traits occur bears a definite relationship to the magnitude of the measurements themselves, just as the errors of marksmanship in shooting

Another way that has been used to measure the excellence or difficulty of a task is by a procedure which may be termed the *method of inverse frequencies.* The general theory of this method is that the excellence or difficulty of a task is some inverse function of the frequency with which it is successfully performed, the underlying assumption being that success and failure are determined by degrees of ability.[1] Concretely, this means that from the per cent of individuals passing or failing a given task, we may infer its difficulty, since by assumption the easier the task the greater will be the number of persons (and the more difficult, the fewer) who will achieve it. This assumption is both based on and supported by the facts of experience. But the validity of the assumption in its general aspects is not enough. The fundamental problem is whether we may reason backwards, and from the incidence of achievement infer its excellence or difficulty. My own view, as already indicated,[2] is that it may not, for the reason that the arguments in its favor lead to a *petitio principii.* Ultimately

---

at a target distribute themselves in certain positions according to the magnitude of their deviation from the bull's eye. The equation of the curve of such distribution expresses the relationship between the frequency of the various deviations, or errors, and the magnitude of these deviations, as calculated from some point of reference (e.g., in the case of the target, the bull's eye). The frequency itself, however, does not define the magnitude of the deviations, much less the relationship of its successive units as such. That is precisely, however, what the transformation of orders of relative position, or for that matter, scores of standard tests in terms of units of variability attempt to do. It is as if from the frequency distribution of errors on a target, one attempted to define the units of length in terms of which they were measured, i.e., the foot or centimeter. No one, of course, would be satisfied to accept such method of defining units of length. One would at least demand that the units thus obtained should be correlated against some others more directly obtained. In the case of mental measurements, the results seem to have a certain validity, because, unlike the case of physical measurements, we have no unequivocally defined units against which to check up our data. In fact, if we had them, there would be no need of employing this round-about method.

[1] And, as Thorndike well points out, "by nothing else."

[2] See above, under remarks on the transformation of measures of relative position into units of equal amount.

one arrives at the same difficulty of having to assume arbitrarily the equality of the units whose equivalence one has attempted to establish. This stricture applies also to the procedure now very much in vogue of defining difficulty statistically, in terms of multiples of the standard deviation, which is only a special case of the method of inverse frequencies.

There remains one more basic method of measuring mental productions quantitatively which needs to be considered. It is *the method of psychophysical correlation.* As the name indicates, its main field of application has been in psychophysics, i.e., that branch of psychology which attempts to study quantitatively the relation of mental to physical processes. The general principle made use of is that of systematic comparison of perceived physical magnitudes with subjective estimates of them, the assumption being that if the latter could be expressed as some mathematical function of the former, one could arrive at some truly objective method of measuring mental processes in terms of units of amount. Suppose, for example, one desires to measure visual ability, more specifically sensory discrimination of light intensity, in such a way that various degrees of this discriminative ability could be quantitatively expressed. To do this, the psychophysicist would proceed in the following manner: He first defines what shall constitute the minimum or least intensity perceived. This, by definition, is the least perceptible difference between any two given sensations of the same kind. In our case it would be the minimum change between two intensities of light such that the subject would be able to perceive that the stimulus was just brighter or less bright than it had been immediately before. This least perceptible difference is then, by assumption, defined as the fundamental unit of sensation. By continuing the process, i.e., having the subject continuously note the moment when he perceives the light intensity change, the experimenter would arrive at a series of sensations differing from each other just by this minimum perceivable amount, i.e., by successive equal units. All that is now necessary is to plot these points against actual measurements of the physical source of stimulation, and find the mathematical relation that exists between the two. The resulting equation gives the permanent definition of the final units.

Several facts regarding this last method will now be noted. The first is the definition of the unit of sensation (or any other mental function that it may be measuring), as a least perceptible difference; the second, that such differences are equal to each other at any point in the scale at which they are perceived, and the third, that these differences can be added. These are not unassailable assumptions,[1] but once they are admitted, it is clear they enable us to do something which the previous methods did not, namely, convert subjective judgments into truly objective measures. For here, unlike in the case of transformations based upon frequency distributions in which the unit of measurement is some arbitrary measure of variability, the measurements now made are in terms of some definite physical unit, such as the second, erg or centimeter. The limitation of this procedure, however, is that the processes measured are the simpler mental functions like sensation and perception, but it is not impossible that with further increase of our knowledge of psychophysical dynamics we may be able to apply this same technique to the measurement of the more complex processes.

[1] The best critique of the psychophysical assumptions will be found in Bergson's Données Immédiates de la Conscience (7). I do not believe that the difficulties are as insurmountable as he makes them out to be. Bergson's conclusion that all sensory intensities are artifacts seems to me to be certainly incorrect.

APPENDIX B

TABLES GIVING MEANS, STANDARD DEVIATIONS AND TOTAL RANGE RATIOS OF HUMAN TRAITS AND ABILITIES, SHOWING THE RANGE AND LIMITS OF HUMAN VARIABILITY

Tables 9 to 15 show how the highest or best individual (as defined in chapter V) compares with the poorest or least endowed individual with respect to any given trait or ability. The figures have been derived from such available measures of human traits and abilities, published or collected within the last thirty years, as meet the statistical requirements set forth in the preceding chapters. These requirements, it will be recalled, are first, that the trait or ability considered must have been measured in comparable units of amount; second, that the number of individuals comprised shall have been sufficiently large for statistical comparison; and third, that the individuals measured shall have been a fairly representative and unbiased sample of the total population which it purported to represent. Unfortunately, only a comparatively small portion of the statistics published in the field of human measurements meets all three requirements. Thus, until very recently most authors in presenting their data contented themselves with mere summary measures of central tendencies, paid little attention to measures of dispersion, and often even neglected to state unequivocally the total number of cases studied. On the other hand, the large amount of statistically refined data which has been collected during the last decade, pertaining to intellectual and educational abilities as measured by various types of mental tests, is almost entirely useless for our purposes, because of the non-comparable character or uncertain equivalence of the successive units in terms of which the abilities are measures.[1] But while these failings have greatly reduced our material, enough is available to enable us to perceive the main facts of human variability and deduce its most probable limits, with a reasonable amount of confidence.

Tables 9 to 15 inclusive in which these facts are summarized are shown on the succeeding pages. They are to be read as follows: Column 1 of each table states the name of the trait or ability and the reference to the source or compiler of the raw data; Column 2, the unit or units in which the capacity has been measured; Column 6, the number of individuals included and a description of the group. The 4th Column gives the average measure,—in nearly all cases the arithmetical mean, of the group; the 5th, the standard deviation of the distribution calculated from the mean.[2] These measures were generally obtainable from the figures furnished by the compiler, but many instances had to be recalculated by the writer from the original data. Column 6 of each table gives what we have defined as the "total range"; it was obtained in one of two ways. The first and usual way was to calculate the equivalent number of cases that would constitute one-tenth of 1 per cent of the total (given in Column 3), and then by simple subtraction (and interpolation where necessary) to determine the limiting points on the scale where the 2nd and the 999th individual per thousand would fall. The scale distance between these two points is the total range. Thus in the case of the stature figures for native white American soldiers (table 9), one-tenth of 1 per cent of the total measured (96,239) is 96; the 96,143 and the 96th individual fall in the class-interval of those measuring 152–153 cm. and 194–195 cm., respectively;

[1] This limitation applies equally to the so-called "T" or standard deviation scales by which many psychologists think they have succeeded in transmuting arbitrary measures into scales with true units of amount but which in point of fact achieve no such thing. See appendix A.

[2] To save space, the probable errors of each of these measures are omitted; all means and S.D.'s are "reliable," that is, are equal to more than 3 times their P.E.'s.

from which by simple calculation their exact scalar position is found to be 194.5 cm. and 152.56 cm. respectively. The total range of the native white southern draft of the United States Army was therefore from 194.9 to 152.56 cm., or 42.44 centimeters.

To calculate the total range in the manner just described it is necessary to have at one's disposal the compilers' original and complete data in the form of a distribution table; also, the number of cases included must not be much under a thousand. Where these conditions are not met, an indirect way of calculating range is still possible providing the form of the distribution is known; and this brings us to the second method for obtaining the total range which I used in a few instances (marked in the tables with asterisks): Where the form of distribution of a series of measures can be assumed to be normal or approximately normal, (and the mean and standard deviation are known) the total range as above defined may be calculated by the formula given in the footnote.[1] I have used this formula in those instances where the distribution tables were not available and where at the same time it seemed likely that the true distribution was not markedly un-Gaussian. On the other hand, where the distribution was definitely skewed and the number of cases under a thousand, but the actual distribution tables available, I calculated the total range in the usual fashion, only using as the limiting cases measures of the 2nd and last but one individual. Thus, for weights of normal hearts (table 13), the total number of cases is 413; calculation of the 0.1th and the 99.9th percentile would give the nonexistent 1/2th and the 412 1/2th individuals; the total range therefore was obtained by taking the difference between the

[1] $R = \frac{L_u}{L_l} = \frac{M + 3\,S.D.}{M - 3\,S.D.}$, where R = the total range ratio, M the mean and S.D. the standard deviation of the distribution. The values of the upper (L_u) and lower (L_l) extremes are of course given by the numerator (M + 3 S.D.) and denominator (M − 3 S.D.) respectively.

measures of 412th and 2nd individuals; these, according to our rule, having become the limiting cases.

The 7th and last column in our tables gives what I have designated as the *total range ratio.* It is the measure which tells us *how many times* greater the capacity of the highest or most superior is to that of the lowest or least endowed individual, and is obtained by dividing the larger by the smaller of the two numbers given in column 7. Since the ratios are pure numbers, we can compare them with one another. They enable us to make such statements as: men vary less as regards stature (table 9) than they do in body weight (table 13); human variability is greater in the case of mental abilities (table 15) than in the case of physical traits (tables 9–12); the best athlete cannot run 100 yards any faster than one and a half times the slowest normal person (table 14); etc. The significance which we may attach to these statements have been discussed in chapters V and VI.

TABLE 9

Range of linear traits

TRAIT OR ABILITY	UNIT OF MEASUREMENT	NUMBER OF INDIVIDUALS AND DESCRIPTION OF GROUP	MEAN	STANDARD DEVIATION	EXTREMES	RANGE RATIO
(57)* Stature (at birth)	Inches	273 male infants (English)	19.69	0.63	22.4 – 18.5	1.21:1
(68) Length of head	Cm.	802 male adults (Egyptian)	190.52	5.90	209.5 –172.0	1.22:1
(68) Breadth of head	Cm.	802 male adults (Egyptian)	144.50	4.67	160.0 –129.5	1.23:1
(57) Stature (at birth)	Inches	209 female infants (English)	20.14	0.74	22.7 – 18.2	1.25:1
(24) Stature	Inches	1,219 females (English), 21–32 years old	63.38	2.46	70.7 – 56.7	1.26:1
(55) Length of leg	Cm.	48,983 Swedish conscripts, 20–23 years old	90.02	4.30	93.1 – 77.3	1.26:1
(88) Stature	Cm.	96,239 white American soldiers	171.99	6.63	152.6 –164.9	1.28:1
(70) Length of femur	Cm.	163 adult males	45.01	2.08	51.2 - 38.7	1.29:1
(24) Sitting height	Inches	1,219 females (English), 17–36 years old	33.94	1.27	28.6 – 37.6	1.31:1
(88) Height of sternal notch	Cm.	97,192 white American soldiers	141.18	5.91	162.0 –123.2	1.31:1
(68) Length of left foot	Mm.	802 adult males (Egyptian)	257.6	12.36	295.0 –223.0	1.32:1
(70) Length of femur	Cm.	124 adult females	41.16	1.94	46.9 – 35.3	1.33:1
(24) Span of arms	Inches	1,241 females (English), 17–32 years old	63.14	2.86	71.8 – 54.5	1.32:1
(88) Span of arms	Cm.	95,596 white American soldiers	175.58	7.95	200.8 –150.2	1.32:1
(68) Length of middle finger	Mm.	802 adult males (Egyptian)	114.09	6.14	134.5 – 99.8	1.39:1
Interpupillary distance	Mm.	529 adult American Negroes	66.4	3.80	77.8 – 55.0	1.40:1
(88) Length of arms	Cm.	82,492 white American soldiers	78.57	4.69	96.5 – 65.2	1.44:1
Mean						1:30:1
Median						1.31:1

* The numbers give reference to the source of the data. For full title, date, etc., of source see "References," at end of book.

TABLE 10

Range of metabolic constants

TRAIT OR ABILITY	UNIT OF MEASUREMENT	NUMBER OF INDIVIDUALS AND DESCRIPTION OF GROUP	MEAN	STANDARD DEVIATION	EXTREMES	RANGE RATIO
(101) Body temperature	Deg. C.	121 normal English girls, 12–13 years	99.13	0.396	100.0 – 98.0	1.02:1
(100) Body temperature	Deg. C.	601 English male convicts	98.38	4.86	99.9 – 96.5	1.04:1
(96) Acidity of blood (H-ion concentration)	H^+ per 10^x ions	Normal adults	−7.4		−7.5 – −7.3[1]	1.29:1[1]
(60) Calcium in spinal fluid	Mg. per 100 cc.	49 male adults	5.01	0.15	5.23 – 4.52	1.16:1
(39) Hemoglobin content in blood (Hb)	Grams per 1000 cc.	40 male adults, 19–27 years	16.06	0.87	18.03 – 14.39	1.25:1
(60) Calcium in blood	Mg. per 100 cc.	72 children, 5–9 years old	10.03	0.23	11.7 – 9.3	1.26:1
(107) Urea in urine	Grams per 1000 cc.	347 French males	21.70		26.21 – 15.90	1.21:1
(6) Heat production	Calories per sq. in.	103 American adult males, 20–23 years	839.38	54.55	930 –706	1.32:1
(97) Duration of pregnancy	Days	245 German women	287.13	14.77	335 –245	1.37:1
(73) Sugar in blood	Mg. per 100 cc.	141 male adults	96.99	6.90	116 –182	1.41:1
(107) Phosphoric acid in urine	Grams per 1000 cc.	347 French males	2.59		2.96 – 2.11	1.41:1
(6) Heat production in 24 hours	Calories per kg.	103 males, 20–32 years old	260.58	22.06	310 –207	1.50:1
(50) Red corpuscles in blood	10^6 per $mm.^3$	112 healthy adults (Swedish), 16–50 years	530.85	61.00	620 –405	1.53:1

(6) O_2 consumption per minute	Cc. per kg.	103 males, 20–32 years old	373.04	32.18	454 –296	1.53:1
(6) CO_2 production per minute	Cc. per kg.	103 males, 20–32 years old	310.52	27.88	378 –245	1.54:1
(50) Blood platelets in blood	10^3 per mm.^{3}	112 healthy Swedish adults	293.97	43.00	390 –205	1.90:1
(107) Uric acid in urine	Grams per 1000 cc.	347 French males	0.501		0.638– 0.334	1.91:1
Mean						1.41
Median						1.37

[1] The numbers 7.5 and 7.3 are logarithms. 1.29 is the ratio between their respective cologs.

TABLE 11

Range in circumference measurements

TRAIT OR ABILITY	UNIT OF MEASUREMENT	NUMBER OF INDIVIDUALS AND DESCRIPTION OF GROUP	MEAN	STANDARD DEVIATION	EXTREMES	RANGE RATIO
(88) Circumference of calf	Cm.	96,087 white American soldiers	34.09	2.02	40.2 –28.0	1.43:1
(88) Patellar circumference	Cm.	96,157 white American soldiers	36.21	1.98	43.5 –28.8	1.51:1
(88) Chest circumference	Cm.	95,867 white American soldiers	88.79	5.18	108.9 –71.4	1.53:1
(88) Neck circumference ence	Cm.	95,874 white American soldiers	35.98	1.80	43.6 –28.0	1.56:1
(88) Thigh circumference	Cm.	95,188 white American soldiers	52.71	3.73	66.0 –42.0	1.57:1
Mean						1.52:1
Median						1.53:1

TABLE 12

Range in physiologic functions

TRAIT OR ABILITY	UNIT OF MEASUREMENT	NUMBER OF INDIVIDUALS AND DESCRIPTION OF GROUP	MEAN	STANDARD DEVIATION	EXTREMES	RANGE RATIO
(31) Respiratory rate	Number per minute	1,028 male adults, 18–21 years (American soldiers)	16.57	1.00	20.0–13.0	1.54:1
(6) Pulse rate	Number per minute	94 newly-born infants	112.18	9.38	140.3–84.0	1.66:1
(6) Pulse rate	Number per minute	116 adult males, 20–24 years	64.4	6.45	83.8–45.1	1.86:1
(31) Respiratory rate	Number per minute	14,442 males, 15–30 years (American soldiers)	18.55	2.88	25.0–13.0	1.88:1
(1) Blood pressure	Hg mm.	1,216 males, 18 years (college students)	130.0	13.4	183.0–87.5	2.09:1
(1) Blood pressure	Hg mm.	1,961 females, 18 years (college students)	117.7	11.0	169.0–83.0	2.03:1
(100) Respiratory rate	Number per minute	255 adult males, 20–24 years (Hungarian soldiers)	15.84	2.35	21.0–10.0	2.10:1
(3) Vital capacity	Deciliters	548 American boys, 59 inches tall	24.91	2.96	34.0–16.0	2.12:1
(3) Vital capacity	Deciliters	632 American girls, 60 inches tall	24.25	3.10	32.0–15.0	2.13:1
(100) Pulse rate	Number per minute	255 adult males, 20–24 years old (Hungarian soldiers)	64.21	8.49	99.0–45.0	2.20:1
(3) Vital capacity	Deciliters	957 American boys, 11 years	21.84	3.42	33.0–12.0	2.75:1
(83) Vital capacity	Cc.	330 adult males, 20 years (Oxford students)	4,278	602.5	6,086–2,470	2.46:1
Mean						2.07:1
Median						2.06:1

TABLE 13

Range of weight of body and its organs

TRAIT OR ABILITY	UNIT OF MEASUREMENT	NUMBER OF INDIVIDUALS AND DESCRIPTION OF GROUP	MEAN	STANDARD DEVIATION	EXTREMES	RANGE RATIO
(70) Weight of brain	Grams	416 adult males (Swedish)	1,400.5	106.33	1,720–1,082	1.59:1
(70) Weight of brain	Grams	233 adult females (Swedish)	1,252.7	100.76	1,555 – 951	1.61:1
(70) Weight of cerebrum	Ounces	308 adult males (English)	41.82	4.46	57.5 – 29.0	1.78:1
(24) Weight of body at birth	Ounces	1,527 male and female infants (English)	112.82	15.04	1,600 – 72.0	2.22:1
(70) Weight of body at birth	Kg.	500 female infants (German)	3.15	0.42	4.41– 1.90	2.32:1
(70) Weight of body at birth	Kg.	500 male infants (German)	3.24	0.44	4.56– 1.92	2.38:1
(29) Weight of healthy heart	Ounces	413 adult males (English)	11.27	3.77	15.2 – 7.1	2.14:1
(29) Weight of healthy kidney	Ounces	413 adult males (English)	12.01	3.98	17.1 – 7.2	2.37:1
(8) Weight of hair	Mg.	100 adult males (Caucasians)	3.10		4.8 – 2.0	2.40:1
(88) Weight of body	Pounds	868,445 white (American soldiers)	141.54	17.82	230.0 – 90.0	2.44:1
(24) Weight of body	Pounds	1,241 adult females ages 17–36 (English)	125.86	17.21	206.0 – 81.0	2.54:1
(51) Weight of placenta	Grams	700 adult females (German)	635.0	123.06	990.0 –400.0	2.48:1
(30) Weight of healthy liver	Ounces	73 adults (English)	57.39	11.26	90.0 – 34.0	2.64:1
Weight of suprarenals		110 foetuses, 39 weeks or over	740.9	251.0	1,450 –400	3.63:1
Mean						2.32:1
Median						2.38:1

TABLE 14

Range of motor capacities

TRAIT OR ABILITY	UNIT OF MEASUREMENT	NUMBER OF INDIVIDUALS AND DESCRIPTION OF GROUP	MEAN	STANDARD DEVIATION	EXTREMES	RANGE RATIO
(26) Extension of wrist	Ang. Deg.	119 French adults	110.9	9.70	140.0 – 85.0	1.65:1
(82) Running 60 meters	Seconds	455 German school boys	9.67	0.87	13.0 – 8.0	1.67:1
(82) High jump	Cm.	500 German school boys, 15 years old	106.01	11.72	141.3 – 70.8	1.99:1
(82) High jump	Cm.	224 German school girls, 16 years old	90.47	10.15	112.9 – 60.0	2.02:1
(82) Broad jump	Cm.	455 German school boys, 15 years old	363.54	41.46	465.5 –225.5	2.07:1
*Speed of inserting bolts	Number in 10 min.	300 boys, 14–15 years old	553.0	83.30	710.0 –340.0	2.09:1
(92) Rotation of eyeball	Mm.	113 adults	35.7	6.10	45.0 – 22.0	2.05:1
(102) Tapping	No taps in 30 secs.	902 American girls, 16–17 years old	153.1	18.54	220.0 –101.0	2.17:1
(102) Tapping	No taps in 30 secs.	1,083 American girls, 16–17 years old	158.4	24.97	230.0 –103.0	2.23:1
*Stringing discs	Number in 10 min.	200 boys, 14–15 years old	41.9	6.20	55.0 – 26.0	2.12:1
(26) Flexion of wrists	Ang. Deg.	190 French adults	117.7	14.02	137.5 – 63.0	2.18:1
(24) Swiftness of blow	10^{-2} secs.	1,360 English females, 18–35 years old	13.7	2.28	20.0 – 7.5	2.67:1
(102) Card sorting	Seconds	857 boys, 14 years old	47.6	8.14	75.0 – 30.0	2.50:1
(102) Card sorting	Seconds	868 girls, 14 years old	44.5	6.34	75.0 – 30.0	2.50:1
(81a) Swiftness of blow	10^{-2} secs.	4,827 English males, 18–37 years old	18.28	2.42	28.6 – 9.0	3.18:1
(80) Latent reflex time (Achilles Tendon)	10^{-3} secs.	80 adult males	53.2	13.35	85.0 – 34.0	2.50:1
(53) Simple reaction time	10^{-3} secs.	113 trained adult males (University students)	199.1	25.50	275.6 –222.6	2.24:1
Mean						2.23:1
Median						2.17:1

* From data made available to author, by director of Vienna Psychotechnical Institute.

TABLE 15

Range of perceptual and intellectual abilities

TRAIT OR ABILITY	UNIT OF MEASUREMENT	NUMBER OF INDIVIDUALS AND DESCRIPTION OF GROUP	MEAN	STANDARD DEVIATION	EXTREMES	RANGE RATIO
(10) Upper limit of audibility	d.v. per second (in thousandths)	156 American adults, 16–30 years	32.29	2.27	42.96– 25.72	1.67:1
(47) Highest audible pitch	d.v. per second (in thousandths)	4,856 English males, 18–36 years	36.10	5.35	50.0 – 20.0	2.50:1
*Memory span for digits (audit.)	Number correctly repeated	236 male adults	6.60	1.13	10.0 – 4.0	2.50:1
(10a) General intelligence (Binet mental age)	M.A. in years	200 English children, 9–9.9 years	9.40	1.24	13.1 – 5.7	2.30:1
(74) Simple learning (Sequin Form Board)	Seconds	172 American children, 11 years	14.89	2.24	23.0 – 9.5	2.42:1
(74) Simple learning (substitution test)	Seconds	150 American children, 11 and 12 years	109.30	24.65	85.0 –165.0	2.85:1
(102) Hard learning (substitution test)	Seconds	766 boys, 14 years	111.8	28.56	232.7 – 60.1	3.87:1
Mean						2.58:1
Median						2.50:1

* Unpublished data of the author.

APPENDIX C

DISTRIBUTION OF TOTAL RANGE RATIOS ACCORDING TO TRAITS AND ABILITIES, AND IN ORDER OF MAGNITUDE

TABLE 16

Range of linear traits

TRAIT OR ABILITY	RANGE RATIO
Length of head	1.22:1
Breadth of head	1.23:1
Stature (at birth)	1.23:1
Length of leg	1.26:1
Stature (adult)	1.27:1
Length of femur	1.31:1
Sitting height	1.31:1
Height of sternal notch	1.31:1
Length of left foot	1.32:1
Span of arms	1.33:1
Length of middle finger	1.39:1
Interpupillary distance	1.40:1
Length of arms	1.44:1
Mean	1.30:1
Median	1.31:1

TABLE 17

Range of metabolic constants

TRAIT OR ABILITY	RANGE RATIO
Body temperature	1.03:1
Calcium in spinal fluid	1.16:1
Urea in urine	1.21:1
Hemoglobin content of blood	1.25:1
Calcium in blood	1.26:1
Acidity of blood	1.29:1
Heat production	1.32:1
Duration of pregnancy	1.37:1
Sugar in blood	1.41:1
Phosphoric acid in urine	1.41:1
Heat production in 24 hours	1.50:1
Red corpuscles in blood	1.53:1
O_2 consumption per minute	1.53:1
CO_2 production per minute	1.54:1
Blood platelets in blood	1.90:1
Uric acid in urine	1.91:1
Mean	1.39:1
Median	1.41:1

TABLE 18

Range of circumference measurements

TRAIT OR ABILITY	RANGE RATIO
Circumference of calf	1.43:1
Patellar circumference	1.51:1
Chest circumference	1.53:1
Neck circumference	1.56:1
Thigh circumference	1.57:1
Mean	1.52:1
Median	1.53:1

TABLE 19

Range in physiological functions

TRAIT OR ABILITY	RANGE RATIO
Pulse rate—at birth	1.66:1
Respiratory rate	1.88:1
Pulse rate	2.03:1
Blood pressure	2.03:1
Vital capacity—age and stature constant	2.13:1
Vital capacity—age constant	2.75:1
Mean	2.07:1
Median	2.06:1

TABLE 20

Range of motor capacities

TRAIT OR ABILITY	RANGE RATIO
Extension of wrist	1.65:1
Running 60 meters	1.67:1
High jump	2.01:1
Rotation of eyeball	2.05:1
Broad jump	2.07:1
Speed of inserting bolts	2.09:1
Stringing discs	2.12:1
Flexion of wrists	2.18:1
Tapping	2.20:1
Simple reaction time	2.24:1
Card sorting	2.50:1
Latent reflex time (Achilles Tendon)	2.50:1
Swiftness of blow	2.93:1
Mean	2.23:1
Median	2.17:1

TABLE 21

Range of weight of body and its organs

TRAIT OR ABILITY	RANGE RATIO
Weight of brain	1.60:1
Weight of cerebrum	1.78:1
Weight of healthy heart	2.14:1
Weight of body at birth	2.32:1
Weight of healthy kidney	2.37:1
Weight of hair	2.40:1
Weight of body	2.44:1
Weight of placenta	2.48:1
Weight of healthy liver	2.64:1
Weight of suprarenals	3.63:1
Mean	2.33:1
Median	2.38:1

TABLE 22

Range of perceptual and intellectual abilities

TRAIT OR ABILITY	RANGE RATIO
Upper limit of audibility	1.67:1
General intelligence (Binet Mental Age)	2.30:1
Simple learning (Form Board)	2 42:1
Highest audible pitch	2.50:1
Memory span for digits	2.50:1
Simple learning (substitution)	2.85:1
Hard learning (substitution)	3.87:1
Mean	2.58:1
Median	2.50:1

REFERENCES

(1) Alvarez, W. C.: Blood pressure in 15,000 University Freshmen. Arch. Int. Med., 1923, 32, pp. 17–30.

(2) Arthur, W.: Relation between Strength of Grip and Certain Mental and Sensory Characters. Biomet., 1924, XVI, p. 399.

(3) Baldwin, B. T.: Breathing capacity according to Height and Age of American Boys and Girls. Amer. Jour. Phys. Anthropol., 1925–29, XII, pp. 261–69.

(4) Baldwin, J. M.: Dict. of Phil. and Psych., Vol. 1, New York, 1928.

(5) Beeson, M. F.: Intelligence and Senescence. Jour. Appl. Psych., 1920, IV, pp. 219–234.

(6) Benedict, F. G., and Harris, J. A.: A Biometric Study of Basal Metabolism. Carnegie Institute, Washington, 1919, Pub. No. 279.

(7) Bergson, H. Données Immédiates de la Conscience. Paris, 1888.

(8) Bernstein, M., and Robertson, S.: Racial and Sexual Differences in Hair Weight. Jour. Phys. Anthropol., 1927, X, pp. 379–384.

(9) Birge, R. T.: Probable Values of General Physical Constants. Phys. Rev. Supplement, 1929, I, p. 22.

(9a) Boring, E.: Physical Dimensions of Consciousness, New York, 1932.

(10) Bunner, F. G.: The Hearing of Primitive Peoples. Arch. Psych., 1908, 2, No. 11.

(10a) Burt, C.: Mental and Schol. Tests. London, 1922.

(11) Cattell, J. McK.: A Statistical Study of Eminent Men. Sci. Mo., 1903, 62, pp. 359–375.

(12) Cattell, J. McK.: The Order of Scientific Merit and the Validity of Votes. American Men of Science, Fourth edition, New York, 1927, pp. 1111–1117.

(13) Cattell, J. McK.: The Distribution of American Men of Science in 1927. American Men of Science, Fourth Edition, New York, 1927, pp. 1118–1129.

(14) Cohen, M. R.: Reason and Nature. New York, 1931.

(14a) Conrad, H. S., Jones, H. E., and Hsaio, H. H.: Sex Differences in Mental Growth and Decline. Jr. Educ. Psychol. 1933, 29, pp. 161–169.

(15) Cooley, C. H.: Genius, Fame, and the Comparison of Races. Annals of Amer. Acad. of Pol. and Soc. Sciences, 1897, XIX, p. 317.

(16) Cornell, B. S.: Pernicious Anemia. Duke University Press, Durham, N. C., 1927, p. 153.

(17) Cox, C. M., and others: The Early Mental Traits of 300 Geniuses. Stanford University, California, 1926.

(18) Cripps, L. C., Greenwood, W., and Newbold: A Biometric Study of the Interrelation of Vital Capacity, Stature, etc. Biomet., 1923, XIV, p. 316–336.

(19) Cruickshank, J. N., and Miller, M. B.: Weight of Foetal Organs. Special Report of Med. Res. Council, No. 86, London, 1924, pp. 33–65.

(20) Cullen, E., and Robinson, H. W.: Normal Variations in Plasma Hydrogen-ion Concentration. Jour. Biol. Chem., 1923, LVII, pp. 533–40.

(21) Cushing, H.: Life of Sir William Osler. Oxford, 1925, Vol. I, pp. 664–685.

(22) Donaldson, H. H.: Growth of the Brain. London, 1899.

(23) Duckworth, D. D.: System of Medicine. 1908, Vol. IV, p. 492.

(23a) Dorland, W. A.: The Age of Mental Virility, 1908.

(24) Elderton, E. M., and Moul, M.: On the Growth Curves of Certain Characters in Women and the Interrelationship of These Characters. Annals of Eugenics, 1928, II, p. 2, pp. 275–336.

(25) Ellis, R. S.: The Psychology of Individual Differences. New York, 1928.

(26) Féré, C.: Varietés de l'amplitude et de la directions de quelques mouvements du membre supérieure. J. de l'Anatomie et de la Physiologie, 1903, XXXIX, pp. 341–352.

(27) Foster, J. C., and Taylor, G. A.: The Applicability of Mental Tests to Persons over 50. Jour. Appl. Psych., IV, 1920.

(28) Galton, F.: Hereditary Genius. Second American Edition, New York, 1891.

(29) Greenwood, M.: Weights of Human Viscera. Biomet., 1904, III, pp. 66–78.

(30) Greenwood, M., and Braun, J. W.: A Second Study of Weight, Variability and Coefficient of Variability of the Human Viscera. Biomet., IX, p. 473.

(31) Gould, B. A.: Investigations in the Military Anthropological Statistics of American Soldiers. New York, 1869. U. S. San. Comm., Sanitary Memoirs, II, Statistics.

(32) Haines, C. J., and Davis, R.: Diabetic Coma with Blood Sugars above 1000 mg. Jour. Amer. Med. Assoc., 1923, 99, No. 1, p. 24.

(33) Harrap, G. A.: Polycythemia Vera. Medicine, 1926, V, p. 29.

(34) Harris, J. A., and Benedict, F. G.: A Biometric Study of Human Basal Metabolism. Proc. Nat. Acad. of Sci. Dec. 1919, 4, pp. 373–376.

(35) Herskowitz, M. J.: Correlation of Length and Breadth of Head in American Negroes. Amer. Jour. Phys. Anthropol., 1926, IX, pp. 82–97.

(36) Hirsch, N. D. M.: Genius and Creative Intelligence. Cambridge, Mass., 1930.

(37) Hollingworth, H. L.: Mental Growth and Decline. New York, 1927, Ch. XIV.

(38) Holzinger, K. J.: Note on the Relation of Vital Capacity to Certain Psychical Characters. Biomet., 1926, XVI, p. 139–156.
(39) Horneffer, L.: Das Blut des Menschen mit neuren Methoden untersucht. Pflüg. Arch. f. Ges. Physiol., 1928, 220, pp. 703.
(40) Hull, C. H.: Aptitude Testing, New York, 1929.
(41) Jackson, C. M.: Measurement of Female Students at the University of Minnesota. Amer. Jour. Phys. Anthropol., 1928–29, XII, pp. 363–413.
(42) Jevons, Stanley W.: The Principles of Science. Eng. Ed., London, 1877. (Reprinted 1913.)
(43) Jones, H. F.: Psychological Studies of Motion Pictures. University of California Publication (Psych.), III, No. 6, pp. 225–243.
(44) Jones, H. E., and Conrad, H. S.: The Growth and Decline of Intelligence, etc. Genet. Psychol. Monog., 1933, XIII, pp. 223–298.
(45) Karshan, M., et al.: Creatine-Creatinine Excretion and Serum Calcium in Normal Male Children. Arch. Ped., 1929, pp. 323–326.
(46) Kastlin, G. J.: Agranultic Angina. Amer. Jour. Med. Sci., 1927, 173, pp. 799.
(47) Koga, J., and Morant, G. M.: On the Degree of Association between Reaction-times in the Different Senses. Biomet., 1923, XV, pp. 346–372.
(48) Köhler, W.: The Mentality of Apes. New York, 1926.
(49) Krehl, L.: Principles of Clinical Pathology. Trans. by A. W. Hewlett, Ind. Ed. Phil., 1907, p. 395.
(50) Kristenson, A.: Studien über die Anzahl der Blutplätchen beim Menchen. Upsala, 1924.
(51) Kruger, R.: In Vierordt's Daten und Tabellen f. Mediziner. Leipzig, 1906, p. 510.
(52) Lazarsfeld, P.: Die Bedeutung der Normalen Verteilungskurve für die Leistungsmessung. Psycho-tech. Zeitsch., 1929, IV, pp. 104–07.
(53) Lemmon, V. W.: The Relation of Reaction Time to Measures of Intelligence. Arch. Psych., 1927, No. 94.
(54) Macdonnell, W. R.: A Study of the Variations and Correlation of the Skull, etc. Biomet., 1904, III, pp. 208–222.
(55) Mahalanobis, P. C.: A Statistical Study of Certain Anthropometric Measurements from Sweden. Biomet., 1930, XXII, p. 94.
(56) Martin, R.: Lehrbuch der Anthropologie. Jena, 1914.
(57) Martin, W. J.: Biometric Studies of the Weight of Infants during the first Days of Life. Annals of Eugenics, 1931, IV, pp. 327–38.
(58) McRae, T.: Ostler's Principles of Medicine. Tenth Edition, New York, 1926, p. 756.
(59) Memoirs of National Academy of Science, Vol. XV, Washington, 1919.
(60) Merrit, J. J., and Bauer, W.: Distribution of Calcium Phosphorous between Cerebrospinal Fluid and Blood Serum. Jour. Physiol. Chem., 1931, 90, p. 21.

(61) MILES, W. R.: Measurement of Certain Abilities throughout Life Span. Proceedings of National Academy of Science, 1931, 17, pp. 627–33.

(62) MILES, W. R., AND C. C.: Correlation of Intelligence Scores, Age, etc. Amer. Jour. Psychol., 1932, XLIV, pp. 44–78.

(63) MITCHELL, F. D. Mathematical Prodigies. Amer. Jour. Psych., 1907, XVIII, pp. 61–143.

(64) MUMFORD, A. A., AND YOUNG, M.: Interrelations of Physical Measurements and the Vital Capacity. Biomet., 1923, XVI, pp. 109–133.

(65) MURRAY, B. M.: The Effect of Maternal and Social Condition and Nutrition upon Birth Weight and Birth Length. Spec. Report Med. Res. Council, No. 81, London, 1924.

(66) MUSSULMAN, J. R.: On the Correlation of Head Measurements and Mental Agility (Women): Biomet., 1928, XVIII, pp. 195–206.

(67) NESBIT, J. F.: The Insanity of Genius. Sixth Edition, London, 1912.

(68) ORENSTEIN, M. M.: Correlation of Anthropological Measurements of Cairo-born Natives. Biomet., 1915, XI, pp. 67–82.

(69) PARSONS, T. R.: On the Reactions of the Blood in the Body. Jour. Physiol., 1917, LI, pp. 440.

(70) PEARL, R.: Variation and Correlation in Brain Weight. Biomet., 1905, IV, pp. 13–104.

(71) PEARSON, K.: Chances of Death. London, 1902.

(72) PEARSON, K.: Skew Variation in Homogeneous Material. Phil. Trans. Royal Soc. of London, Series A, 1895, CLXXXVI, pp. 314–343.

(73) PIERCE, H. F., AND SCOTT, E. L.: Variations in the Reducing Power (Sugar) of Normal Blood. Arch. Int. Med., 1928, Vol. 4, pp. 586–600.

(74) PINTNER, R., AND PATERSON, D. G.: A Scale of Performance Tests. New York, 1917.

(75) POINCARÉ, H.: Science et Methode. Paris, 1909.

(76) POINCARÉ, H.: La Valeur de la Science. Paris, 1905.

(77) POINCARÉ, H.: La Science et l'Hypothese. Paris, 1906.

(78) QUETELET, A.: L'Anthropometrie. Paris, 1871.

(79) RILEY, W. I.: Theories of Genius. Jour. Phil. Psychol. and Sci. Meth., 1905, pp. 345 et ff.

(80) ROUNDS, G. H.: Is the Latent Time of the Achilles Tendon Reflex a Criterion of Speed in Mental Reactions? Arch. Psych., 1928, No. 95.

(81) RUPP, H.: Über Haufigkeitskurevn. Psychotech. Ztsch., 1929, IV, pp. 90–104 and 119–138.

(81a) RUGER, H., AND STOESSIGER, B.: Growth Curves of Certain Characteristics in Man. An. Eugen., 1926, I, Pts. 1 and 2, pp. 67–110.

(82) SCHIOZ, CARL: Massenuntersuchungen über die Sportische Leistungfähigkeit von Knaben U. Mädchen der Hoheren Schulen. Berlin, 1929.

(83) SCHUSTER, E.: First Results from Oxford Anthropological Laboratories. Biomet., 1911–13, VIII, p. 40 and ff.

(84) SCRIPTURE, E. W.: Arithmetical Prodigies. Amer. Jour. Psychol., 1891, IV, pp. 1–59.
(85) SPEARMAN, C.: The Abilities of Man. New York, 1927, Ch. IX and XXI.
(86) SPITZKA, E. H.: A Study of Brain Weights of Men Notable in the Professions, Arts and Science. Phil. Med. Jour., 1903, XI, pp. 757–760.
(87) STILES, C. W.: Memory Tests of School Children. Pub. Health Reports. Washington, D. C., 1915, pp. 3738–3745.
(88) Statistics, Medical Department of the United States Army in the World War. Vol. XV, Part I, Army Anthropology. Washington, 1920.
(89) THORNDIKE, E. L.: Mental and Social Measurements. Second Edition. New York, 1916.
(90) THORNDIKE, E. L.: The Measurement of Intelligence. New York, 1928.
(91) THORNDIKE, E. L., ET AL.: Adult Learning. New York, 1928.
(92) TRAVIS, R. C.: Experimental Studies in Ocular Behaviour. Jour. Gen. Psychol., 1932, VII, pp. 311–325.
(93) TURCK, H.: Man of Genius. London, 1914.
(94) THURSTONE, L. L.: The Absolute Zero in the Intelligence Measurement. Jour. Ed. Psychol., 1928, 19, pp.
(95) THURSTONE, L. L., AND ACKERSON, L.: The Mental Growth Curve for the Binet Tests. Jour. Ed. Psychol., 1929, 20, pp. 569–583.
(96) VAN SLYKE, D. D.: Studies in Acidosis. The Normal and Abnormal Variations in the Acid Base Balance of the Blood. Jour. Biol. Chem., 1921, XLIV, pp. 157–176.
(97) VIERORDT, H.: Daten und Tabellen für Mediziner. Third Edition, Leipzig, 1906.
(98) WECHSLER, D.: The Range of Human Capacities. Sci. Mo., 1930, XXXI, pp. 35–39.
(99) WECHSLER, D.: On the Limits of Human Variability. Psychol. Rev., 1932, XXXIX, pp. 87–90.
(100) WHITING, M.: A Study of Clinical Anthropology. Biomet., 1915, XI, pp. 1–49.
(101) WILLIAMS, M. H., BELL, J., AND PEARSON, F.: A Statistical Study of Oral Temperatures. Studies in Nat. Deterioration, No. IX. Drapers Co. Research Memoirs. University of London, 1914.
(102) WOOLEY, M. T.: An Experimental Study of Children. New York, 1926.
(103) World Almanac. New York, 1910, 1913, 1932.
(104) WILDER, B. G.: Jour. Nerv. and Ment. Dis., 1911, 38, No. 2.
(105) WERTHEIMER, M.: Studies in the Theory of Gestalt. Psychologische Forschung, 1923, IV, pp. 301 et ff.
(106) YULE, G. M.: Introduction to the Theory of Statistics. Sixth Edition, London, 1922.
(107) YVON ET BERLIOZ: Composition Moyenne de l'Urine Normale. Rev. de Med., 1888, VIII, pp. 713–18.

INDEX

Sans Tache

Sans Tache

IN THE "elder days of art" each artist or craftsman enjoyed the privilege of independent creation. He carried through a process of manufacture from beginning to end. The scribe of the days before the printing press was such a craftsman. So was the printer in the days before the machine process. He stood or fell, as a craftsman, by the merit or demerit of his finished product.

Modern machine production has added much to the worker's productivity and to his material welfare; but it has deprived him of the old creative distinctiveness. His work is merged in the work of the team, and lost sight of as something representing him and his personality.

Many hands and minds contribute to the manufacture of a book, in this day of specialization. There are seven distinct major processes in the making of a book: The type must first be set; by the monotype method, there are two processes, the "keyboarding" of the MS and the casting of the type from the perforated paper rolls thus produced. Formulas and other intricate work must be hand-set; then the whole brought together ("composed") in its true order, made into pages and forms. The results must be checked by proof reading at each stage. Then comes the "make-ready" and press-run and finally the binding into volumes.

All of these processes, except that of binding into cloth or leather covers, are carried on under our roof.

The motto of the Waverly Press is *Sans Tache.* Our ideal is to manufacture books *"without blemish"*—worthy books, worthily printed, with worthy typography—books to which we shall be proud to attach our imprint, made by craftsmen who are willing to accept open responsibility for their work, and who are entitled to credit for creditable performance.

The printing craftsman of today is quite as much a craftsman as his predecessor. There is quite as much discrimination between poor work and good. We are of the opinion that the individuality of the worker should not be wholly lost. The members of our staff who have contributed their skill of hand and brain to this volume are:

Keyboards: Katharine Carr, Mary Franck, Gene Sandberg.

Casters: Kenneth Brown, George Bullinger, Norwood Eaton, Charles Fick, Martin Griffen, Henry Lee, Mahlon Robinson, George Smith, Ernest Wann.

Proof Room: Helen Defibaugh, Dorothy Fick, Alice Grabau, Betty Hagins, Angeline Johnson, Ruth Kelley, Henry King, Audrey Knight, Mary Reed, Alice Reuter, Catharine Robinson, Evelyn Rogers, Shirley Seidel, Louisa Westcott, Virginia Williams.

Composing Room: Emerson Medairy, John Flanagan, Paul Franz, Preston Gatton, Harry Harmeyer, Harold Hoover, Emory Hopkins, Ray Kauffman, Charles Smith, Ernest Salgado, William Sanders, Andrew Rassa, Anthony Wagner, Vernon Thomas, Harry Pullara.

Press Room: Thomas Shreck, George Lyons, Fred Lucker, August Hildebrand.

Folders: Laurence Krug, Clifton Hedley.

Cutters: William Armiger, William Heatterwich.